Cal Coolidge

doesn't live here

any more

glimpses of Northampton

and other spots in the Pioneer Valley
and further afield

With thanks to the
DAILY HAMPSHIRE GAZETTE
of Northampton, Mass., in whose pages
these columns first appeared.

TEDDY MILNE

PITTENBRUACH PRESS   Northampton, Mass.

ISBN: 0-938875-33-7
LCCC: 94-74079

First printing 1994
10 9 8 7 6 5 4 3 2 1

Published by PITTENBRUACH PRESS
15 Walnut Street
PO Box 553
Northampton, MA 01061-0553

Cover photo: Main Street, Northampton
by Teddy Milne

1

All my life I've been bent on trying something new, stretching out, reaching up, moving on. Who would ever have thought I'd be back in Northampton, Mass., doing a weekly column for the Gazette, after being so long away? Yet I have a feeling of rightness about it, of having finally resolved a long-time inner conflict between having roots and having wings.

Mobility is part of the American character. After all, our forefathers left the familiar for an unknown New World, and succeeding generations pioneered to the west. It's in our blood as well as in our tradition.

Even today, what family do you know that does not have distant brothers, far-off daughters? We are always ready to pick up and move in order to find something better, or even just something different.

As a child, like many another preacher's kid, I moved every two years, growing up in a variety of Maine villages and Boston suburbs, never able to name a real "home town."

But even in this valley awash with peripatetic students, you can find under the surface a bedrock of community, stability, roots, if you know how to recognize it. I didn't.

I came to Northampton by pure chance. I had been living in Cambridge for a number of years, but one day on the subway I suddenly decided I'd had it with the smell of stale chewing gum, the flashers on the Common, and the screech of streetcar wheels at

Boylston Street station. I had lived in the city long enough. I would head west -- but not too far.

I drove out to look over Williamstown. When I came through the Pioneer Valley I liked what I saw, and after looking at Williamstown, I circled back. I can't say I've been here ever since, but I seem to keep returning.

If I'd known how to put down roots, I probably would have done it when I started working at the Gazette, those years ago. A reporter gets to know nearly everybody, picks up the general drift of the local political and social structures, and has entree to all kinds of organizations, committees, free lunches, and press parties.

But I hadn't a clue how putting down roots was done. Perhaps I also shied away from the idea of getting tied down. I still had itchy feet, even after several years of travel around the US, Europe, and North Africa.

When I married Alec Milne, general manager of WHMP, I was welcomed even further into Northampton life. At one point we counted up that Alec was on 22 political or civic committees. He even ran for mayor, but lost that one.

I never actually quit the Gazette; I took a leave of absence to have a baby. Then we bought Greetings, the little hole-in-the-wall card shop that had been started by John Hurley and his wife, and became fixtures on Main Street.

But proof that there were no deep roots was that we went off to Scotland for a visit, and stayed eight years.

Scotland held family ties for Alec, but not, I thought, for me. Yet that's where I started learning about community.

Several generations of the same family lived in close proximity -- not always in close harmony, no -- and in that slower paced, deeply-rooted community I began to remember that I too was part of the planet, and not just an onlooker.

Even then, I might have felt wary of growing too attached to a place so far from my native land, but I got shoved.

My genealogist brother sent me a family tree, and to my amazement, I learned that one of my English ancestors had been involved in destroying the village in 1303.

I never dared tell anyone -- 1303 is not that long ago in Britain -- but the realization that an ancestor of mine had walked on that particular bit of earth made it seem legitimate that I put down some roots.

And I found I liked it. It didn't clip my wings after all, it just gave me surer footing when I landed.

When we came back to Northampton (Florence) after eight years in Scotland, Alec tried to nudge me back to the Gazette, but I wasn't ready. I was still homesick for Scotland, that kinder, gentler nation. I had learned how to take root, but I hadn't yet learned how to get transplanted.

Now I live in downtown Northampton, in a neighborhood where houses are closer together and there is more of a sense of community. There are actually pedestrians here, and cats sit sunning themselves on old-fashioned porches. After a snowfall, everyone foregathers on the sidewalk with shovels and greetings, and in the summer radios blare for backyard barbecues. The neighborhood store sells penny candy to the kids, and customers hang around discussing the weather.

And here, after all this time, maybe a tentative root or two has probed the well-mowed earth. Maybe that's why, after 22 years on a leave of absence, writing for the Gazette appeals to me again.

2

A story in the Gazette about the former Frontier Pharmacy in South Deerfield got me to thinking about how I happened to wind up in Northampton.

It was all because of an ice cream cone and a stuck door.

I've mentioned how I got sick of the city and decided to head west.

Down at the corner gas station in Cambridge there was a van for sale, just the thing for moving. When I went down to ask about it, the owner was filling someone's tank, and some gas spilled onto the ground. The driver asked belligerently, "You're not going to make me pay for what's on the ground, are you?"

The garage owner answered, "It's yours. Pick it up." And handed him the bill. The driver swore, but paid up.

I doubted that I was a match for this tough guy, so I was surprised when I got the van for only $60. And that it actually ran.

I packed up my two little kids and we set off to explore the wilds of Western Massachusetts. I was in a holiday mood, glad to be leaving the city, and we meandered across the countryside.

We stopped in South Deerfield for an ice cream cone at the Frontier Pharmacy. The cones cost a third of what they had in Boston, the counter clerk was friendly, and there were several quasi-customers hanging around telling jokes. I had forgotten what living in a small town could be like. I was charmed.

I drove dutifully on out to Williamstown, to North Adams, to Pittsfield. But they just couldn't compete with South Deerfield and the Pioneer Valley, and that friendly drugstore.

The ice cream cone drew me back to South Deerfield for another look. A month later we were living in Sunderland, in a small apartment at Alec Kulessa's.

I had, truly, forgotten what living in a small town could be like. I didn't know anybody. The only fun spot was the library. I was the only pedestrian. There was no such thing as a job.

No doubt it's different now, but then the only thing to do seemed to be to move yet again. I began to look for work in both Greenfield and Northampton. Wherever I got a job, I decided, there we would live. But nothing much was going on in Greenfield.

I finally got a job teaching French at Northampton School for Girls, and we moved to Franklin Street in Northampton. After teaching there for two years, a spot opened up on the Gazette staff; I kept my ties with NSFG through editing their Alumnae News and doing public relations for them, until their merger with Williston.

And the stuck door? I didn't realize until several years later that the stuck door was what had determined our fate. One day at the school Miss Bement started talking about her hiring methods. "The door to my office always got stuck," she said. "I decided to leave it that way, and hire people on the basis of what they did about it."

So it wasn't my brilliance in French that had impressed her and led us to Northampton, but what I had done about her door? What a let-down.

And what had I done about her door, anyway? I

racked my brains, and finally a dim and rather disturbing memory returned.

I had kicked it open.

Well, it must have been the right thing to do.

3

I drove by the old Northampton School for Girls campus on Pomeroy Terrace last week. I guess I shouldn't have been surprised at how things have changed in the thirty-odd years since the school merged with Williston Academy and moved to Easthampton.

Actually, I had gone to look for a tree, the one planted while I was there in the 60's, to replace the elm that had once shaded the gracious lawn.

I couldn't find the tree. I couldn't even find the lawn. Did it used to be where the parking lot now is?

And where was the angelus bell, and the sundial? Where were the girls in white dresses, carrying flowers, marching to graduation through the rose arbor? I think I caught a glimpse of them, in my memory's eye.

I worked for Northampton School for Girls in several capacities, those many years ago: first as a teacher of French, then later as publicity director, then as editor of the Alumnae News Magazine, and as advisor to the school newspaper, "Pegasus." The memories are still strong, and pleasant.

Off in a corner of Northampton, the school may have seldom impinged on the rest of the city -- with the possible exception of the annual Summer School of French, when every student was supposed to speak nothing but French, even while in town.

Certainly the Ding Dong man was accustomed to halting French phrases from the girls on Pomeroy Terrace, although he seemed a bit more bemused, or perhaps bemented, when school head Miss Bement issued forth a more complex demand. We were all impressed, not only with Miss B's French, but with the ice cream man's patience and fancy guess-work.

Then there was the senior-faculty hockey game, for which I had innocently volunteered, completely forgetting it had been too many years since I had last played, and that I hadn't been much good at it even then. I wheezed my way through, but just barely.

I didn't learn not to volunteer, though. A few years later I was one of the chaperones to go to New York with a group of seniors to see a Broadway play, visit the UN and other places of interest. It was a lot more fun playing hooky than playing hockey.

Not only was the play (Hadrian VII) fun, but during intermission I met a Northampton friend's mother and an old college friend from Boston whom I hadn't seen for years. I thought Manhattan was too big a place to make that kind of connections.

Some of us met another person, too, in the lobby of our hotel -- Mohammed Ali himself. Surrounded by admiring teenaged girls, he wasn't stinging like a bee that day. In fact he obligingly autographed my box of flash bulbs.

But Mohammed Ali is getting pretty far afield from the staid serenity, the never-ending politeness, the happy chatter and girlish giggling, of Pomeroy Terrace.

Miss Whitaker and Miss Bement certainly had what it took to start and run a girls school for some 40 years. With a combination of tough strength, sweet reason, and impregnable integrity, they nurtured and encouraged two generations of young women, nearly half of them day students from this area.

It's impressive, I think, that the school's stated objectives were not only to prepare students for college, but also "the development of womanhood, of well-adjusted personalities, of intelligent and sympathetic interest in world affairs, of the spirit of service to the community, and of love of learning."

It's difficult nowadays to find any school at which similar aims are even mentioned, much less believed in. I wonder sometimes: will we ever see their like again?

4

A recent crossword puzzle contained the word "crony," not a word one sees often nowadays, but one which has the odor of city hall smoke-filled rooms to me. My Websters' only says "a close friend of long standing," so the political overtones must be out of my own experience.

It seems harder to detect close friendships among men nowadays, but 20 years ago it was still occasionally to be seen, and perhaps the best example I remember was the friendship between Ed O'Dea and Chick Murphy, both long gone now.

Chick was Northampton's postmaster, and Ed was managing editor of the Gazette, back in the days when those two offices stood cheek by jowl on Armory Street. Both Ed and Chick were big, Irish, homely, and popular, and they were in the best sense of the word, cronies.

Chick would pop into the Gazette newsroom at least once a week. He was always the first one in town to know a good new joke, and he would come over to boom it out across the clatter of typewriters. Ed would heave with silent laughter, and the rest of us would guffaw in various keys and decibels. Then the two would talk politics and go out to lunch.

Ed was a peach of a guy to work for, and knew everything that was percolating under the surface in Northampton. Like Chick, he kept his hand in the political brews in town and was active in civic organizations. He also became a probation officer in addition to managing the Gazette.

I remember when President Kennedy was coming to Amherst to speak in 1963, we got a dated release about the event. The release date meant that our arch rival, The Springfield Union, would beat us to the story, as usual. Ed got on the phone to Washington, talking to everyone he knew and everyone THEY knew and finally got the story from another source, which meant that (as far as he was concerned at least) we could go ahead with the story a day early. How Ed crowed! Nothing pleased him more than getting a scoop on the Union.

This makes it even more remarkable that he was a crony of Chick's, because Chick started out as a newspaperman and had been in charge of the Northampton office of the Springfield Union back in the 1930's.

I knew Chick primarily as the Postmaster, but he played major roles in the YMCA, the Three County Fair, the Democratic City Committee, the Elks scholarship program, and a number of other organizations. He was an ardent athlete, playing semipro baseball and basketball, coaching at the Y and St. Michael's High School. He was an alderman (before we had a city council) and on the School Committee, leading the fight for a new high school. A John F. Murphy Achievement Fund for Northampton kids was set up after his death.

There was one characteristic of Chick's that we in the Gazette office found fascinating. When embarrassed, he would turn a frighteningly deep purple.

And once we found out that Jean Sheehan, a reporter whose desk was next to Ed's, had a very similar trait (perhaps a redder shade of red), the rest of us took perverse delight in getting the two of them embarrassed. As the blood rose in their faces, a whoosh of delighted "O-o-oh's" would rise with it. We shouldn't have done it, but it was too great a temptation.

But looking back, it wasn't the blushing that was remarkable, it was the depth of friendship and the shared commitment to public service. I hope people nowadays aren't so caught up in making a buck that they are missing out on what Ed and Chick represented: being valued and important members of their community and, best of all, enjoying that with a crony.

5

When I was working for the Gazette I met quite a few notables. Politicians used to come in to the office to make friendly noises -- they probably still do -- and we would be introduced to people like Robert and Ted Kennedy, Ed Brooke, who was a senator those days, and various Massachusetts governors.

When Elizabeth Taylor came to town to make the movie "Who's Afraid of Virginia Woolf" on the Smith College campus, some rivalries blew up on the staff. Bernie Decker, who said he wouldn't cross the street to see Elizabeth Taylor, was the one assigned to go and write up her move into the house they had rented up in the hills. He did it -- but from across the street, so he could keep his word.

Liz didn't want to be interviewed, and that was that. I got back from vacation and found that nearly everyone on the staff had tried, and failed. It had become a touchy subject, and apparently a closed one. Or was it? Life Magazine called my then fiance, Alec Milne, at WHMP, and requested him to ask her two more questions as follow-up to an interview she had already done with them. He called me and asked if I'd like to go along.

"Sure," I said, but knowing the rivalry in the office over this non-story, I thought I'd better ask our editor diplomatically.

"IF," I said to him, "IF I should get a chance to get in to see Liz Taylor, is there anything you'd like me to ask her?"

"Butt out!" he said, or words to that effect.

It didn't matter, because the star refused to see my husband anyway.

When Julie Nixon was attending Smith, and David Eisenhower was at Amherst, the only time I saw them was at a Republican fundraiser, just before they left. Whenever I let my husband go alone to St. John's Episcopal Church, Julie would go, and vice versa. Not once did our attendance coincide. My kids saw her -- but they were far more interested in the secret service men.

When Jack Kennedy came to give his talk at Amherst College, there was no way most of us could go. I had to be on the office end of a phone, in order to take down the news before we went to press. It was touch and go, since Kennedy arrived nearly an hour late, stretching our already stretched deadline to the limit. The photographers, especially, were going crazy. We got our story -- but Alec was over there actually shaking hands with Jack. It wasn't fair!

One day, though, I finally got my chance at interviewing a celebrity. Someone tipped off the Gazette that Jimmy Cagney was in town, attending the Morgan Horse Show. I was sent up to a motel in Hatfield, where he was reputed to be staying, but though I knocked on every door, no one was on the premises.

Just in case, I visited every other motel in the area, too, but it was no dice.

Finally giving up, I drove back down Route 5 to Northampton. When I stopped for the light in the middle of town I happened to look over, and there he was, sitting two feet away in the next car.

"Jimmy Cagney, right?" I said, afraid the light was going to change any minute.

He nodded, looking harrassed.

"Here for the Horse Show?"

He nodded again, barely glancing at me.

"I hope you'll enjoy it."

"Thanks."

The light turned green, and they shot off. I didn't even have a chance to get him to do his "you dirty rat" routine.

Sparse though it was, I wrote it up -- the shortest interview on record, at least for me.

It was almost as short as the conversation I had with Spencer Tracy in Stockholm. I was walking down the street when I spotted him having his picture taken in front of the Grand Hotel. Not wanting to interrupt it, I hesitated.

"Let the little Swedish flicka go by," Tracy said, smiling and waving me on.

I was so elated at being taken for a Swedish girl -- the equivalent of being thought beautiful -- that I didn't even tell him I was from Boston. I just walked on by, grinning from ear to ear.

6

Not since the 60s has there been this much activity at the NASA Space Center at Cape Canaveral, Florida. A successful space shuttle last month, and now another one due to go up next week. Is the Gazette sending down a reporter?

You think I'm kidding, right? Did you know that the Gazette had a reporter at several of the Apollo moon shot blast-offs? All right, so it was just a coincidence that my mother lived two miles from Cape Canaveral (sometimes Cape Kennedy), and that we had made it a tradition to go down every April.

My husband Alec and I both had press cards (he as general manager of WHMP) and we would write to NASA for passes to the liftoffs.

The press, of course, had prime space at Cape Canaveral. The one great advantage, which turned into a disadvantage at the climactic point, was that we had a cantilevered roof over the press stand, keeping out the worst of the blazing Florida sun.

The problem was that when the Apollo rose up beyond the roof line, suddenly reporters from above and behind us would come leaping down through the maze of wires in order to keep it in sight.

If you've ever seen a herd of reporters on the stampede, you'll know we had to get out of the way pretty smartly.

The most unforgettable part of any lift-off is the sound. There's some primordial instinct in us that makes us want to run away from a loud noise.

And that roar coming toward us across the lagoon is so earth-shaking, so enormous, and so unending that, without our veneer of civilization, we would all take to our heels.

You are sure in some inner corner of you that you won't be able to stand the vibration, that the earth will collapse with it. But there's no place to go, so you stand there with the hair rising on the back of your neck, learning about adrenalin, until miraculously the roar begins to fade and the "bird" is rising majestically against the blue sky. Perhaps the adrenalin is one reason for the wild jubilation that follows.

There were reporters from all over the world there. We met journalists from Germany, Japan, the Netherlands, Australia; and at the bank of microphones you could hear two dozen languages at once.

The question these foreign newspeople always asked us was, "Why aren't Americans more interested in the space program?" We never had an answer.

One of the most colorful reporters was Mary Bubb, who wrote for the Cocoa Beach paper and had covered every liftoff. Her writing was unsophisticated, but she had made a place for herself. She took to making a new hat for each launch, with pictures of the astronauts and cutouts of each flight's mascot.

One, I remember, was Caspar the Friendly Ghost. The hats got bigger and more exotic with each flight, and even if you knew no-one else, you knew who SHE was!

The photographers, poor things, had no shade. They lined up along the lagoon, wilting -- and occasionally wading, in spite of the alligators. The view along that line was impressive; there must have been a million dollars worth of camera equipment, telephoto lenses and filters, in that row.

Behind them was ABC's neat little machine, an automatic tracking camera that I believe cost $1.3 million.

Off to our left was the row of network trailers. A few days beforehand, we visited the CBS one, and I got a picture of my husband at Walter Cronkite's desk (there was a marker that said "belly button here.") Behind it a picture window got the full view of the Apollo in its gantry, out across the lagoon.

In fact, my husband met Walter Cronkite in the men's room at one liftoff, and came back beaming. I was rather annoyed that I had not also gone to the men's room!

But when Alec told me "some photographer" had taken their picture together, I put on my Sherlock Holmes hat and went after it. All Alec had learned, thrilled as he was by actually talking to Cronkite (mainly about Cronkite's son at Deerfield Academy), was that it was a local photographer. And, oh yes, she was a woman. I called all the local papers and finally located a woman photographer in Titusville.

Yes, she had taken the photo. Sure, she'd send me some complimentary copies. They now have pride of place in our photo album.

At one of these liftoffs, the public address system kept announcing the arrival of VIPs at the VIP stand, a couple of miles away (with no roof).

They also announced that a couple of buses would go over to the VIP stand and return in time for the liftoff. Naturally Alec and I went. I was on the trail of the Russian poet, Yevtushenko; Alec wanted to see Connie Stevens. Yevtushenko never materialized, but Alec got a photo of me looking over Connie's shoulder.

We were standing in line, sweating, to get some soft drinks when the man in front of us pointed over to the press stand and said to his wife. "That's where the REAL VIP's are, over there." Come of think of it, yeah. We left the Florida sunshine and went back to the shade.

One of the Apollos we saw go up was Apollo 13, the one that had a "problem" and almost didn't make it back. As soon as one of these "birds" goes up, control passes to Houston, so most of the reporters flew there. As an alternative, I went in to the Cape Kennedy press office every day and picked up bulletins. The office was quiet, nearly empty, and rather dismal in those breath-holding days.

Even the main street of Cocoa Beach had mournful-looking signs about coming back safely. And you heard on the radio every day, "This time we almost made it to the moon, didn't we girl..."

We drove home before the end of the story, and my son Tim, who was in Kennedy Junior High at the time, wanted to have the complete set of documents. I encouraged him to write to NASA and they were kind enough to send him the rest. We still have a box full of those Apollo 13 press bulletins somewhere in the attic.

Would you believe I keep a camera that doesn't work, just because the case has an Apollo 13 sticker on it?

Anyway, to get back to my question, is the Gazette sending a reporter down? Just checking.

7

It's with some surprise that I realized the other day that there can't be many people still around who remember Sidney Smith, the man who started the Gazette Christmas toy fund.

Sid Smith was business manager of the Gazette back in the days when it was housed in a much smaller building on Armory Street. When I was a reporter and copy editor there (and occasionally city editor pro tem), our editorial office was to the right of the front entrance, and the business office -- which consisted of Sid Smith and Kathy Hurley -- was to the left.

Newspaper offices in general have changed in the last 20 years. The Gazette, the Boston Globe, and doubtless many others, have left behind the cramped, Dickensian little offices that were the legacy of earlier days, and moved to large open spaces with cubicles, word processors, and flourescent lights.

Even the newspaper in our sister city, Northampton England, which formerly had an even tinier space than ours, is now in a large, modern building on the edge of the city. One tradition that persists there, however, is the lack of wastebaskets. Papers just get tossed onto the floor, where from time to time a janitor moves it along with a long-handled broom. And I'm talking about huge clumps of it, not just popcorn balls. But reporters seem to wade through it without noticing.

There may be advantages to modernization, but, like new cheese, some of the flavor has been lost. Those crowded, rather dingy little offices, where Bob Cratchit would not have been out of place, lent themselves to a kind of empathy and hilarity that may be less evident today.

Sidney Smith, to get back to our former business manager, was already partly retired when I worked there across the room from his desk. He would come in, do a little work, and then wander around waiting for the paper to come off the press. He would read it thoroughly, and then go home.

He started the toy fund in 1934, during the depression, when so many families were finding it hard to make ends meet. Hmm. As the French say, the more things change, the more they stay the same.

Like most reporters, I took my turn at writing the daily account of how the fund was going, getting information from Children's Aid and Family Service about needy families, and from Sid Smith about the amount collected. Over the years the fund has risen from the first year's $200 to last year's $29,581 (with another $3,600 donated by the Gazette to make up a deficit).

Sid, a teddybear of a man, could be a trifle somnambulant during most of the year, but he always came alive during toy fund season. His gruff manner hid a generous heart, and that glowed through at Christmastime. He had a Santa Claus look about him then, or perhaps a better analogy would be a reformed Scrooge, full of the milk of human kindness but a little uncomfortable with it.

In some ways Sid was the rock on which the Gazette rested -- always there, always solid, always dependable -- while we reporters buzzed in and out on our erratic errands.

I remember one day he was sitting across from me at an empty desk, reading that day's newly-printed paper. I watched as the paper gradually folded inward and his head fell forward. Then with a jerk he woke up, and, avoiding my eye, he carefully finished the job his nap had started -- he crumpled the paper up into a ball as if that had always been his intention, and tossed it into the wastbasket. Then, with great dignity, he got up and went over to get another copy.

One day my four-year-old, Peter, had been sick in the night and I took him to work with me. I was working on a picture page, and after showing Peter what I was doing, I gave him some paper and a pencil. He decided to do a picture page, too.

Sid, who was always attracted to children, came over to watch. Peter had made several squares and was carefully drawing a picture in each one.

"What's that a picture of?" said Sid, indicating one of the squares.

"Half a horse."

Sid shook with silent laughter.

"And what's that one, then?"

"The other half of the horse."

This time Sid laughed so hard he had to wipe his eyes.

They talked some more, and Peter was as intrigued with Sid as Sid was with Peter. As Sid finally walked away, Peter turned to me.

"When you die, can I work here?" he asked.

That's the kind of effect Sid Smith had on people.

I'm sad that for many people Sidney Smith is just a name on a toy fund, but glad that his name does indeed live on, attached to a project that was close to his heart.

8

Local politics is gearing itself up for another election, and the battle seems pretty mild compared to some others we've seen. Earnest letters to the editor, full of bright promises. Maybe some not-so-nice statements which are called hard-hitting by one side, and cheap-shots by the other. Photographs and baby-kissing and hand-stroking and telephone calls -- it's all part of the excitement, the business, the glitz of politics.

It always seems a shame that elections don't prove who is the best person to be in government, but only who is the most charming, the most charismatic; or possibly who has the most cash or the fewest qualms. The one who knows best how to manage the media, manipulate the voters, stage the drama, is the one who wins, while the people often lose. In any case, whether it's Northampton, Mass., or Washington DC, the voter is then promptly forgotten until the next time around.

Local politics, when I first started poking my nose into it as a Gazette reporter, seemed relatively harmless. But even then there were some interesting twists by native sons.

I remember one city council meeting where the mayor of the time felt the vote wasn't going quite his way. So he voted once to make it a tie, and then voted again to break the tie. Somehow or other his logic won the day, though I've never figured out how.

Another time, the mayor had his team all set up in advance. Something was on the agenda that he didn't want discussed, just passed. So in double-quick time the conversation went something like the following:

"Proposal #8A?"

"Move to accept."

"Second the motion."

"All in favor -- motion passed."

"Move to adjourn."

"Second the motion."

"Adjourned."

"Hey, wait a minute..."

"Sorry, we're adjourned."

It was breathtaking. At least it left me breathless.

But perhaps the strangest event was a Memorial Day when the city fathers marched through town to Bridge Street Cemetery, where the mayor gave a speech.

Those were hard-line anti-Communism days, and it was no surprise when he got onto that topic. But at one point people started drifting away, and he kind of lost his head. Suddenly he shouted out, "We have to fight the enemies of Communism!"

He had our attention then. Alec and I looked at each other, murmuring, "Could he have said what we think he said?"

But most people, including the mayor, didn't even notice. I guess it doesn't really matter what a politician says, as long as he keeps talking.

Once I wrote an article that the county commissioners didn't like, and they started going into executive session (illegally) when I walked in the door. I started getting black looks from reporters from other papers, who were out in the cold along with me. Giving the full story in the Gazette was just making the commissioners angrier. So I phoned

Ed Brooke, who was then our state attorney general, and he said he'd look into it. Came the next county commission meeting, and they all knew about the phone call. Gee, how did that happen, and in Massachusetts? I really got it that day.

I forget what made it come out all right eventually, but I do remember that in the end the two oldest commissioners, now long gone, leaned across the bench and kissed me. Those were more forgiving times.

A trick used a few times in the School Committee in those good old days went like this: A motion would pass, five to four. Then someone would move that the acceptance be made unanimous. This would also pass five to four.

In a later meeting, if one of the recalcitrant four spoke up against the proposal, one of the five was sure to say, "But you voted for it. It's in the record, look: passed unanimously."

Can you imagine the frustration, the rage, that would fill the room?

I guess the point is that a politician who plots things out ahead of time is likely to have an advantage over us poor suckers.

Which is one of the best reasons I ever heard for putting some effort into keeping an eye on City Hall, the State House, the Congress. The price of democracy is higher than we think; it isn't won by simply voting now and then, but by "eternal vigilance" over those we send into power.

9

The mayoral primary got me thinking about a former Northampton mayor, Durbin Wells. I think he was the last Republican mayor we had -- though if he was running today I doubt if he would be Republican any more; he not only liked broccoli, he wasn't afraid of admitting to the L-word.

Durb died in 1984, but his name still brings a smile to those who knew him. He was that rarity, a man who didn't take himself too seriously.

He attended Choate with Jack Kennedy and his brother Joe, played -- could it have been football? -- at Amherst College, served in the Pacific in the US Army during World War II, went into the insurance business, wrote for the Gazette and the Springfield Daily News.

He was also busy in volunteer things: singing in local choral groups, working for the Amherst College Capital Fund, becoming director of the Community Chest and president of the Northampton Area Council of Churches.

Then in 1964 he took his son, Durbin Jr., then age 16, down to a civil rights demonstration in North Carolina, and got arrested. He wrote movingly about the experience and got some national attention for the movement. I don't think he was ever quite the same after that.

After his one term as mayor of Northampton, he went to fund-raise for Old Sturbridge Village, and became vice president of the organization. In spite of all these achievements he often spoke of himself as if he were a failure. Not one to brag, our Durb.

Then in 1972 he had a stroke, and retired back to Northampton with his wife, Jane. For the next 12 years it was a daily struggle.

When we came back from Scotland, I went to see them. Durb could walk with a walker by then, and I suggested I take him out to lunch, both to give him an outing and to give Jane a break from care-giving.

It became a weekly adventure, and our only quarrel was who was going to pay for lunch. It was always a delight to talk to him, because he cut right through any pretense or pussyfooting, right to the heart of things.

These outings were a direct result of my years in Scotland. A friend in Aberdeen was running an afternoon "club" for stroke patients there, and one day she told me someone had asked if there couldn't be a similar club up our way. Would I start one?

It took a few weeks to get things organized -- a place to meet, helpers, finding stroke patients who were interested -- but eventually we began. Since few of the ten or so members had transportation, we would even pick them up, and became adept at squeezing wheelchairs into the trunks of mini cars.

There were two men, John and Hutch, who couldn't speak, but they came faithfully every week. That is, Hutch could say yes and no, that was about it. John hadn't spoken for 20 years, even to his wife Jessie.

Though the club was also supposed to give relief to care-givers, Jessie regularly came as one of the helpers. They even got John back into speech therapy, and she got her reward a couple of years later, just before he died, when he broke his long silence with a slow but clear "I love you."

While the rest of the group played word-recognition "bingo" or other games John and Hutch played checkers. Every now and then they would both shake with quiet laughter -- we never knew why, but all of us would laugh with them, pleased to see their pleasure.

We'd all have the inevitable cup of tea and a few cookies, for which we asked them to donate ten pence so it wouldn't taste of charity.

When we came back to this country, I missed John and Hutch and the others, and taking Durb to lunch was a pleasant way to keep on.

In our culture we don't see many people in wheelchairs. They're hidden away, and you have to really seek them out. Yet it's worth it. I learned a lot from Durb and my Scottish friends.

Perseverance, for one thing. I often think I would probably just give up if something debilitating happened to me. I'm not at all sure I'd have what it takes, as Durb so definitely did, to keep going, to stay cheerful, to become even more considerate of others, to not give up.

As someone said at Durbin's memorial service, "If his dreams failed, he upped and dreamed new dreams." To me, that's a rare art.

10

A number of winters ago I was standing at the window of our then house on Bridge Road in Florence, looking out at a backyard covered with snow. But the snow had an asterisk on it -- paths worn through the white stuff, from front to back by my son Tim and his friend Art Donahue who lived over on Hastings Heights; diagonally from corner to corner by the Paklewski and Lenkowski boys who lived in those quadrants. But what was that path that went across from left to right?

It took me a few days to realize it was the beagle who lived next door with Bud and Ruth Arnold, doing his daily reconnaissance.

That back yard saw a lot of comings and goings, changes both seasonal and ongoing. Flower and vegetable gardens that grew and were abandoned; maple trees to be climbed; slapstick baseball games, an archery range, a climbing frame that, when the boys outgrew it, became the scaffolding for picking cherries. A big truck-tire sandbox came and went. A hammock, though greatly appreciated, went up only one summer.

The boys gave neighborhood carnivals to raise money for Muscular Dystrophy and the YMCA, built their soap-box derby cars, and learned how to split wood there during our wood-stove era.

Barbecues and picnics, midnight star-gazing, meteor showers and aurora borealis treats; fruit trees, flowering bushes, an occasional rabbit, tomato plants, croquet games, treasure hunts, all took their turns.

And oh yes, lots of lawn-mowing, leaf-raking, and snowman building through the seasons.

Some of the neighbors were a little amused at our garage, when Alec built a shed on the back, and then added a shed onto the shed, and then a lean-to onto that. But the boys learned carpentry and house-painting on those sheds, so they had their uses.

The reason that back yard came back to mind was seeing Art Donahue's name as cameraman on a show emanating from one of the Springfield television stations. Art and Tim shared an interest in photography and movie-making, and Art, at least, became a professional. It's nice to have some visual evidence that he's still around and has made a name for himself.

One of their first cinematographic ventures, though, was an epic drama called "Blood in the Paint," starring half the neighborhood and containing several scenes of rather innocent pre-teen gore.

I don't remember the plot, if there was one, but I do remember how horrified Alec and I were. No, it wasn't the blood, it was when we realized that our unthinking son had a disembodied hand reaching slowly behind the pot -- and removing from its hiding place our back door key, in front of the entire neighbor-hood.

We were rather put out that we had to abandon a perfectly good spot and find a new place to hide it.

It's a little strange to think that all those neighborhood kids have grown up now, and may have kids of their own; that those paths don't exist any more, and that the friendly neighborhood beagle who left as distinct a mark as the boys, is long gone.

I see one or other of the old neighbors now and then, and once in a while I drive down that way, though it saddens me to see the cherry trees gone.

I miss the backyard, though. Criss-crossed paths aren't all I can picture there. There are echoes of laughter, visions of first baby steps on the grass, photos of family picnics, remembrances of competing with the blue jays for the cherries. A place for lazing.

I don't laze any more. It's all work, work, work. But you knew that, right?

11

Sailing has always fascinated me. The ingeniousness of being propelled by the wind, rather than having some man-made contrivance push you, makes me feel in tune with nature. Also, I'm the kind who likes sports where you can sit down.

I started my sailing career in Boston, at the Community Sailing Club, on the Charles River Basin. The club was started originally for newsboys, and then expanded to include any kid. Anyone under age 18 paid 25 cents a month back then, and I was out on those murky waters of the Charles several times a week during the summer.

When I got to be 18, and the price went up to $25, I switched allegiance to the M.I.T. Yacht Club across the basin. My brother worked at M.I.T. and I managed to finagle my way in on his good name. The yacht club taught us more refinements than I had learned at Community, and in fact it took me a whole summer to pass the helmsman exam.

What held me up was trying to throw a length of rope 40 feet to land on the back of a chair. It was one of those great achievements that are never any use to you afterwards.

We had races at M.I.T., and although I wasn't keen on racing I often ended up being coopted as crew. Many days were so airless the races were a joke, but there were other days when the crew was hanging by the knees over the water to keep the boat from overturning. That was exhilirating.

When we moved out to the Pioneer Valley, I

bought a sailboat from a fellow journalist, and took it out on the Connecticut River (precarious), Paradise Pond (hilarious), and Highland Lake (various).

Seeing that a lot of kids were taking out sailboats on Highland Lake and bumping into one another, as well as other dangerous practices, I thought it might be a good idea to set up some races, which could also introduce racing rules and teach the kids better boating.

My two oldest sons had meantime built a sailing raft. We bought two long logs, and the kids nailed boards across to make a small deck. An old canvas tent made a sail, and a small tree was the mast.

We set out two marker buoys (plastic milk jugs tied to cement blocks) which the racers would have to go around for a three-leg course.

The day of the first race arrived. My husband fell in and had to be rowed ashore. The kids took off on the raft, got to the first marker, and kept right on going -- they couldn't turn it! They ended up in a swamp at the far end of the lake and had to be towed home.

But it was great fun for all. We had several races that summer, and only one of them was canceled. I kept saying it was too windy, and the kids were all arguing with me, when across the lake came a small catamaran.

It was really creaming along in the wind, and the kids said, "See that? It's a great day for a race. Come on!" Just then the catamaran somersaulted forwards, turning completely upside down in the water. Everyone rushed to their rescue, and the kids backed off. Maybe it WAS too windy, after all!

Despite all my experiences, I began to think my sailing career was jinxed. The first trip of the season, at any rate. On those first trips I've had masts break in two, rudders fall apart, fittings break loose, centerboards rot out, and I've even got caught under bridges and run into rocks. I'm glad I wasn't carrying any oil.

I think my sailing days are over, but I still have some lovely memories: waking aboard a sailboat and seeing a grey heron in the pink mist of sunrise, framed in the porthole; manoevering through the tidy river towns of the Norfolk Broads; swooshing down North Sea waves outside Cullen Harbor in Scotland; sailing under the Golden Gate Bridge; taking the helm of a huge catamaran in Bermuda; watching a lunar elipse from aboard ship in the Virgin Islands; sailing through thousands of islands in the dark near Stockholm, and even tacking endlessly around the island in Paradise Pond.

As Toad says in "Wind in the Willows," "There is nothing, absolutely nothing, half so much worth doing as simply messing about in boats." Amen to that.

12

If you were around here many years ago, you may remember seeing an old pink stationwagon with a canoe sticking out the back, a red kneesock tied to the bow.

That was us. Before we ever bought the sailboat, our canoe "Thisldu" took us on a great adventure down the Connecticut River.

It started out innocently enough. The kids and I used to put the canoe in at Sportsman's Marina and paddle up to Elwell Island for picnics and wading.

Then one day the current was too strong to go upriver, so willy-nilly we went down, finally beaching it on the Hockanum side and walking back.

The canoe was a heavy one with sponsons on the sides to prevent tipping, and there was no way we could get it up that steep bank, so we decided that the next day we'd retrieve it and paddle on down to a better landfall.

By the time we reached the Oxbow, I was hooked. This new view of the place we lived in was too fascinating to give up. I was all for going on down to Long Island Sound, in easy stages. The kids would play Indians, Huck Finn, and pirates along the way.

Bob and Gladys Myers from Williamsburg were avid canoeists, and began joining us every weekend with their own light-weight canoe. We made frequent stops, at every island and sandbar, at every marina, wherever there was a fisherman or other sign of life. At first we'd take the canoes back home every night, but as we got further from Hamp, we began camping along the shore overnight, borrowing a tent from some Leverett friends.

It was eerie to paddle through Springfield and hardly even know it was there, and satisfying to slip under busy bridges and to wave at trains. The boys learned fishing from an African-American man near Agawam, dug for buried treasure on Blackbeard's Island, learned how to paddle a canoe, set up a tent, and gather firewood.

When we got to the Holyoke Dam, we hauled the canoe out and put it in below all the white water. But when we got to Hartford, it was a different story. The Myers in their canoe and we in ours pulled over to the bank, which was extremely steep and tall. We got their canoe up the narrow path, but there was no chance we could do the same with the heavier Thisldu.

The alternative was to enter the canal, but the canal keeper said he couldn't let a canoe in, only larger boats. It seemed to be an impasse, but I kept on talking, and finally it became clear that the problem lay in the locks at the lower end of the canal. There were several of those, and it was too expensive to fill and empty them for one small canoe.

Aha, but we could take the canoe out of the canal where it ran alongside Route 5 in Windsor Locks. In that case, couldn't he let us into the first lock, which was already level with the canal?

I think he was rather pleased that there was a solution. He opened the lock, and Thisldu and the Myers (who had returned) entered the canal.

The canal was a revelation, so calm and serene and undisturbed. And then, even more fascinating, we were suddenly paddling down a wooden viaduct, built high above a brook. We could look over the sides, down to the perpendicular brook running beneath us.

The kids, however, seemed more fascinated with Bob remaining upright as we paddled under the low bridges in Windsor Locks, his hat just missing the steel girders, while the rest of us cowards ducked.

Where the road drew near the canal, we pulled the canoes out and went across the street to Friendly's for an ice cream cone. We had become canawlers, and needed to celebrate.

The next weekend we drove the canoe down to Wethersfield Cove to continue downriver. We emerged from the cove to a swiftly running current which carried us along without paddling. It was great, until we suddenly rounded a bend in the river and saw tall buildings up ahead. There wasn't supposed to be a city here, was there? We kept on paddling until it became crystal clear that this was Hartford. We had been going upriver, with the tide!

In fact, the tide was so strong that we had to wait for it to turn before we could go on. It was embarrassing to be hanging onto a piling when a covey of campers came paddling past, slipping easily downriver in their lighter-weight canoes while they looked at us pityingly.

One night we stopped at a sandy beach just above the Portland-Middletown bridge, and set up our tent. We were talking with some beachcombers when we all became aware of a humming noise getting louder and louder. What was it, traffic on the bridge at that hour? We were puzzled for a few minutes, until the answer manifested itself. It was mosquitoes, thousands of them. We ducked into the tent and stayed there.

It didn't help that we had to get up at 5 a.m. to catch the morning tide. The borrowed tent was still black with mosquitoes when we folded it up, and I wondered if it would ever be the same again. I felt guilty, but didn't know what I could do about it. Poor tent, that's not all that was going to befall it.

In the tidal waters below Hartford, the boat traffic was beginning to become worrisome. Not only were there weekend motorboaters, there were also ocean-going oil tankers, whipping up waves that were sometimes hard for a canoe to negotiate. When we got to East Haddam, and found we had to cross the now-wide river, I had to paddle like mad to make it across between tankers.

We tied up the canoe and went to find something to eat and phone for a friend to pick us up. When she arrived, we went back and found the tide had come up over the canoe, completely soaking all our sleeping bags, the tent, and all our other equipment.

Amazingly, the tent's owners are still friends.

With one of those lightning decisions for which other people are more usually famous, I pointed out that we had come upriver from the Sound to East Haddam on a commercial boat trip, so that we had actually "done" all the river from Northampton to the Sound. Maybe it was time to quit.

It wasn't our last voyage. A bunch of us drove up to Gill and floated down to Turners Falls, trying to finish off the Massachusetts part of the river and nearly missing a wedding in the process.

More recently, I canoed with some colleagues from the Deerfield River to Sunderland (where the canoe tipped over, giving us a ducking and a good laugh).

There's still some of the river to do, but old Thisldu was sold long ago and I'm not sure I'm up to all that heavy paddling any more. Maybe I was right to quit while I was ahead.

What a contrast it is, though, between the New Jersey Turnpike, where I find myself far too often, and the calm serenity of the river. All journeys have their fascination, but in these days of stress, noise, gas fumes and cement, give me a river any time.

13

It must be 20 years since the last Soap Box
Derby racer rolled down the hill by Smith's School.
There were a lot of good things about the idea
of the Soap Box Derby. It challenged the kids,
created community spirit, brought good publicity to
the sponsors. Our two teenage sons entered the Derby
one year, and I think learned a lot from building
their cars.
Even our three-year-old enjoyed the project.
He'd put on a helmet and sit in a cardboard box going
"vroom vroom" for hours on end. In fact on the day
of the race, a couple of smiling officials lifted
Jamie and his box over to the ramp, much to his great
glee. He leaned forward, eyes gleaming, prepared to
go to the bottom of the hill. But when the gate went
down, the cardboard box stayed where it was. What
disappointment!
Businesses in town paid for the basic kit, which
included wheels, brakes, and steering. The kid himself, with no parental help (I think advice was
okay), had to build the chassis.
Building those cars took an amazing amount of
time, thought, energy, and perseverance for our sons,
and it was good to see them growing in the process.
Not only learning how to build something, but also
how to plan ahead, overcome obstacles, solve problems, get past discouragement, take care of tools
and paintbrushes, stick it out, get it done on time.

Then came the event itself. It was like a carnival: sunshine and cheers, parents with cameras, running children and dogs, balloons and banners, hot dog and ice cream vendors. The kids lined up their racers in the DPW yard, where they were all inspected to make sure everything was safe and within the rules.

A ramp had been built up in the middle of the road in front of Smith's School, with two hinged gates at the foot of the ramp. Two racers were rolled up to the gates, and when the starting gun went off and the gates went down, the motorless racers would roll off the ramp and on down the hill. A flat-bed truck brought kids and cars back up the hill.

The kids raced two by two, and each one was assigned to two races. This is where I started to see defects in the plan. All these kids had arrived with high enthusiasm, a sense of accomplishment, and dreams of glory. But the way things were set up, every single kid, except the one winner, was doomed to taste defeat, to go home a loser. Even the winner was likely to lose in the state semi-finals or national finals.

After such a lot of hard work, it was all over for most of the contestants in just a few minutes.

Now, there are always people who will argue that competition is a good thing. But there are degrees of good, aren't there? For instance, if the kids had been divided into two teams, 50 percent of them could have been winners instead of just one -- rather a large step forward.

Or perhaps they could have called it a rally instead of a race; let each kid have six turns on the hill, trying to beat his or her own time instead of somcone else's.

Then the cars could have been lined up at the DPW yard so people could admire, parents could take pictures, kids could exchange information on what they had done, what had worked and what hadn't worked, so that next year they could have made improvements.

With a presentation of badges or certificates and everyone's photo in the paper, they could have all ended up with a sense of accomplishment instead of one of defeat.

In any case, that year the Soap Box Derby movement collapsed. It turned out that the national winner had cheated.

Maybe it was to be expected, when the emphasis was on winning rather than on the challenge and fun of building one's first car. One dishonest kid was enough to ruin the fun for thousands of communities.

If fun it was.

14

The Alaska oil spill, nuclear plant leaks, toxic pesticides in apples and grapes, permanent smog over Mexico City, widespread pollution in the USSR -- environmental problems are world-wide and getting worse. Not many people nowadays can ignore the subject. But how serious about it are we?

I have to hand it to my son Tim. Back in the days when nobody was paying much attention, Tim made me stop using the dishwasher and dryer, put bricks in the johns, and dragged me all over New England while he made a film on recycling. All this before he was sixteen.

He started -- or was at least a prime mover of -- the Ecology Action Club at Northampton High School, and his group provided the volunteer labor when Northampton had its first "Recycling Day" May 1, 1971.

That experiment brought in three tons of glass and five tons of newspaper, and the proceeds from the sale of this detritus was given to the Hamp High club, which turned it over to the school department to help buy air pollution devices for school boilers.

These were serious kids.

After several other recycling days, the project gradually grew into the full-time collection center for glass, newspaper, and aluminum that we have on Locus Street today. The center also has a trash compactor, which can save trips to the dump.

Speaking of dumps, have you ever seen one from the bottom up? When I was chauffeuring Tim around to film incinerators, junk compactors, and landfills (complete with clouds of seagulls), I also took him down into the then-new landfill dump on Glendale Road.

If you've been out to the Northampton dump lately, you'll know you now have to drive up a mountain to get to the current trash area. But in those days, you drove down, WAY down, into a huge pit. I drove the station wagon to the bottom, with three or four boys in the back, and after a filming session we got in to start back up. But our wheels only spun around in the sand.

I had visions of having to leave the car there, never to be seen again, but with some pushing from the boys, and luck, we got it moving. I didn't dare stop for the kids, but kept on going until I had something more solid under the wheels. Tim and his friends had a long climb back up to the surface.

It turned out to be a darned good movie, which Tim sold to the Northampton school system (still available for viewing there, as far as I know), and to Maine television. If he had pursued it, it could have had a much wider audience, but typically for Tim, he went on to other projects.

His environmental efforts didn't stop with the USA. He was also responsible for Great Britain's first Earth Day, April 27, 1973. He and some cohorts at Buckie High School in Scotland proclaimed the day, and Tim saw no reason why it should be limited to Buckie. Our family was going on a trip around Britain at the time, and we took along an armload of posters. Every time we came to a town, Tim would jump out and tape up a poster.

That made it an all-Britain event.

I'm not sure the Brits were really ready for this, but nevertheless he was interviewed on the BBC and collected news items from all around the country, most of them concentrating on the idea of putting bricks in the toilet (or cistern, as they said over there). One wit combined two of Earth Day's ideas and suggested putting bricks in the yard and planting a tree in the cistern.

April seems to be the time of year for thinking about trash. Spring cleaning, maybe? The Locust Street recycling center has been going since April 29, 1972, and has not only increased the longevity of the landfill, it has also often paid for itself and even earned money for the city, though not every year.

It's also THE place to be on a Saturday morning, for meeting people you haven't seen in years. And don't forget there's free sand for icy driveways.

See you there.

15

Has it ever struck you as strange that we celebrate "Labor" day by not going to work?

We ex-Puritans don't celebrate labor all that
much at any time. A large part of the American dream
is to strike it rich enough (preferably in the lottery rather than through work) so that we can sit
around with nothing whatever to do.

This in spite of our childhood, when we had that
kind of vacation and were bored out of our skulls.

I'm no different. For years my holidays have
been either working vacations when I caught up with
those least-enjoyed tasks I'd been letting slip by,
or else they were long, exhausting trips with all the
housework but none of the labor-saving devices.

Did people call trips "exhausting" before they
invented combustion engines? Did they know how
ironic it would become when they coined the phrase "a
driving rain?" Did they suspect that "holy-days"
would become the time people were least likely to go
to church?

We were quite logical when we abandoned the word
"holiday" and chose "vacation," which comes from the
same root as "vacant." What we long for most, it
seems, is a vacant mind. We don't often achieve it.

Last week out in California, though, I re-dis-
covered the hammock.

You can't do much of anything in a hammock. You
can't even drink lemonade without a few contortions.
The people sitting at nearby tables, who feel com-

pelled to talk, will talk to each other and leave you alone.

I just lay there under the pepper tree, rocking gently in the ocean breeze, watching the heat waves rise over Disneyland, admiring the little mid-air ecstasies of the humming-birds.

I remembered with great pleasure the one summer we got the hammock up in our back yard in Florence. There it was cherry trees, cardinals, and the smell of cut grass and mower fumes, but the feeling of leisure was the same.

Maybe it's because everyone knows how hard it is to get out of a hammock, but whatever the reason, the hammock person is never the one who is asked to go get some more lemonade or to turn off the sprinklers or phone the theater. There is nothing whatever to do except watch the clouds drift by. Your brain even slows down. It's a small, quiet world of its own.

But there's something in New England air that makes one suspicious of such leisure. Returning home from Bradley Airport I was telling the bus driver about the perpetual beach party that seems to go on along the California coast: bonfires, surf boards, bikini-clad silhouettes against the sunset, the sound of Springsteen and laughter.

"It doesn't seem right," he commented, his voice thick with longing.

I think we're afraid that old rocking chair, old hammock, old free and easy life, is going to get us. We'll forget how to go back to work. And when it comes right down to it, we like to get things done, to keep busy, to make things happen.

Don't we?

16

For years the only PVTA bus I was familiar with was the bus that goes to Amherst. It's mainly a student bus, and the conversations you overhear are about dates, restaurants, exams, professors.

But recently I've had occasion to use another bus, the one labeled King Street or Florence, and the flavor and mood are entirely different. It's rather intriguing to suddenly find that there's a mobile community traveling around the city, that you didn't know about.

The route meanders around town, hitting almost all the spots anyone would need to go to -- Thorne's Market, Calvin Theater, the old Armory, McDonald's, Stop and Shop, Jackson Street School, Hampshsire Heights, Caldor; right through Meadowbrook, with its speed bumps, to Straw Avenue; the Silk Mill, High Street and the housing for the elderly there; Florence Center, Florence Heights, back to the center; Kaiser Permanente; back the same way to Northampton center, then down Pleasant to Wright Avenue, Wally Salvo House, and the Academy. And it's free all year.

You want to go to the library? The stop at the Academy is a block away. The hospital? Well, forget that one, unless you want to walk down Hatfield Street from Bridge Road.

But it's surprising how much of the city it does cover. Most, if not all, of the housing projects; good shopping areas; two medical facilities; and

Florence, which I used to think was only attainable on the infrequent Williamsburg bus, for seventy cents each way.

The atmosphere on the bus is lighter and cozier, too. Everyone seems to know everyone else, since childhood. There's only one bus, trundling around its route once every hour, so the regulars have a friendly relationship with John, the usual driver, greeting him by name, exchanging jokes.

On the first of the month, the bus is more than usually full. A woman with gray hair shows John a photograph, taken in 1897, of her father on a motorcycle. "Wow," says John, who takes a few seconds to look it over thoroughly and ask questions. The photo is handed around the bus as John pulls out into the traffic.

"Can you let me off at Wendy's?" Sure.

A man swings on and gives John a newspaper clipping. John thanks him with enthusiasm. "Told you I'd find it," says the man as he takes a seat.

A woman gets on with a load of washing, heading for the laundromat near Big Y. A neighbor asks if she'll do his laundry, too, and there is some good-natured bantering.

The bus turns into the parking lot, stops in front of Stop and Shop.

"How long have I got?" asks a departing shopper.

"Thirty-eight minutes and thirty seconds," John answers without hesitation.

Two more clamber down, and the next man to get off repeats, "You say we've got thirty-eight minutes and thirty seconds?"

"Not any more. It's 20 seconds now." They both laugh.

In the back two women talk in rapid-fire Spanish. If they can talk that fast, doesn't that mean they have to think that fast, too? I'm full of admiration.

A woman gets on with a baby, another passenger helps with the folded-up stroller. Nobody pushes, no-one's in a hurry. Even the teenagers seem well-behaved. "Can you let me off at the corner?" Sure.

Next day at Thornes' Market, I sit down on the bench outside.

"Waiting for the Florence bus?" a man asks shyly, and when I say yes, he smiles. As if I've got to be okay if I'm a member of that close little community. He joins me on the bench, and we wait in the sunshine.

17

Living in Northampton, with Smith College just up the street, I've sometimes decided to sit in on a course there. It's a very small fee for the privilege.

The first course I audited this way was mineralogy. I had always envied people who could pick up a rock on the beach and say "Ah yes, muscovite schist."

I still can't identify rocks on the beach, but I may sound a little more knowledgeable in gem shops.

One of my strongest recollections from that course was of a curious Smithy asking me why I was taking it. "For the fun of it," I said. She looked totally blank. I guess it wasn't fun to her.

Another year it was a course in criminology. I had already suffered through criminology in my college days, but a blind friend who was taking the course needed a seeing-eye dog and I was elected.

Criminology at Smith, I'm happy to report, was much livelier than the course I took at Boston University, some years ago.

At Smith, the first task the instructor gave us was filling out a questionnaire that listed 30 or 40 commonly-broken laws, including such no-nos as cheating on your income tax, illegal parking, speeding.

After checking off the ones we had broken, we swapped the questionnaires around for anonymity. Everybody in the class admitted to having broken at least two laws, and one had put down 27 (was she kidding?).

The moral of the story was, to paraphrase Pogo, that we had met the criminal and he was us. The only difference between us and them was that we hadn't got caught. From then on we had a little more trouble talking about "them" as different and separate from ourselves.

The books were exciting, too. One, "No One Will Lissen" (that's how it was spelled) was about kids -- mostly black kids -- caught up in the juvenile court system.

Most of us, without really thinking about it, want criminals to be put away somewhere, out of our way, so we'll be "safe," and so we won't have to think about them. In the juvenile system, kids who had no acceptable place to live were sometimes jailed for really minor offences, just because there was no room anywhere else to put them. And in the juvenile system, one isn't sentenced to a fixed length of time. Kids can stay in an institution until they're 18, for stealing an apple. "Les Miserables" are still with us.

I hope things have improved since I took the course, but I somehow doubt it.

This time I decided to take a course in musical composition. So far I've managed to keep the professor from realizing how little I know. What will happen when he finds me out? Meantime I sit there with serious music students who have studied the cello, flute, viola, since they were six years old.

All I can claim is that I must have at least HEARD more music than they have. I've had a few years' head start.

I've learned one interesting fact already. I called up the college to ask where I could park, and the answer was, "You can't." What spaces there are barely accommodate faculty and staff, and students have to just lump it. For someone as paranoid as I am about getting parking tickets, that's bad news. Maybe I'll write a song about it.

There's one other post-teenager in the class, who drives about 20 miles to attend. He's already done some composing, but the professor told him "Now we have to bring you into the 20th century." We may get dragged into it together, kicking and screaming.

The first day in class, one student from Hampshire College talked himself out of being there, because he "didn't know enough." But then, he wasn't taking it for the fun of it. College can be such a deadly serious business.

But auditing -- that's a pleasure.

18

One of the nice things about living in a big
city is the drama of the streets. Boston, for
instance: a violinist in Park Street Station, Brother
Blue telling stories in Harvard Square, a jazz trio
on Newbury Street -- street theater, mimes, clowns,
musicians and storytellers.

Even Northampton, although it couldn't be char-
acterized as a BIG city, has some moments of delight
and charm. A classical guitarist sitting on a bench
outside Thornes Market in the summertime. Michael
Cooper on his stilts, walking nonchalantly down
Bridge Street from twelve feet up. A big man riding
by on a tandem with a small teddy bear strapped to
the other seat. Those nursery school wagons blos-
soming with little kids. And a man called Owl.

Perhaps he chose me among the passersby because
I was just dawdling along in the middle of town. I
could see that he was going to ask me something, and
I presumed it was going to be "Where's the library"
or some such thing.

That was the first surprise.

What he asked was, "Do you like poetry?"

I laughed self-consciously and looked him over.
Dressed warmly for winter, he reminded me of a blond
and bearded version of Robin Williams.

"Sure," I said, wondering if he was selling
books.

"Could I tell you a poem? Then if you liked it,
you could give me a small donation."

This time I laughed outright, in delight. "I can't give you much."

"That's okay." He waited.

I hovered between curiosity and suspicion. Would his poem be any good? Would I be bored? Would he expect too much money? Shouldn't I get on home? But curiosisty won out.

"All right, then, go ahead."

Yet another surprise -- it wasn't just a recitation, it was a performance. Real storytelling. His eyes lively with humor, his gray mittens weaving about in the air, he spun color, fantasy, and magic forests right before my eyes.

I'd never been a sole audience before, and there was something enchanting about it. It makes you feel like someone special -- makes you KNOW you're someone special.

With a surprise ending that made me laugh, the gray mittens stopped weaving their spell. Was he poet, a storyteller, or a magician? All I knew was, it had been well worth the wait.

As I was digging into my wallet I got nosey. "Do you do this all the time?"

"Yep."

"Make a living at it?"

"Yep. Not bad."

"That's very entrepreneurial of you! I admire that. I guess I'm an entrepreneur myself." We grinned at each other.

Still feeling enchanted, delighted, special, and grinning from ear to ear, I started to walk away, then turned back. "What's your name?"

"Owl."

It figured. "Thanks, Owl."

I walked on down Lower Main Street. The sun looked brighter, people looked friendlier. What a difference it makes to a dull day, to run into the unusual, perhaps especially so in a place with a prosaic name like Main Street.

I hope you meet him, too.

19

Did you hear the wail of bagpipes near Dryads Green on Monday? No, it wasn't your imagination, nor the dryads coming back to cavort: two pipers from the Berkshire Highlanders Pipe Band came along to help a group of us celebrate Scotland and plan future Scottish events.

The hosts for the evening were the minister at First Church, Peter Ives, and his Scottish wife, Jenny Fleming. You may know by now how tickled I am by connections, and with Peter and Jenny those connections fly thick and fast.

Not only our common love for Scotland. It also turns out that Peter's grandmother was my godmother.

Hilda Ives was a well-known woman minister some years ago, and a friend of my mother, who was also a woman minister in the days when these were rare birds. When my mother began studies at Andover-Newton Theological School, we first moved into Hilda Ives' apartment, as she was away most of the time. Earlier, we had stayed briefly with Hilda's mother in Portland, Maine. I was in a canoe-tilting contest with Peter's cousin as a child.

Then there's Williston Academy, where Peter taught and his father had been chaplain; at about the same time, I was publicity director at the sister school, Northampton School for Girls (which is now part of Williston).

A more astonishing connection is Singapore, where my parents were missionaries and so were

Jenny's, though not at the same time. Other missionaries, however, were friends with both families -- for instance close college friends of my parents, whose son and I have corresponded off and on over the years.

At present, though, the Scottish tie is uppermost. The get-together at the Ives' house included not only the pipers -- both their music and their humor were a delight -- but also some Robert Burns poems, recited by Robert Tunnicliffe and James MacRostie, and a "Toast to the Immortal Memory;" some slides of Scotland (including two of the Loch Ness monster); reminiscences of Burns Suppers, happy feasts which take place around the world on January 25 (including Northampton); and a discussion about joining the international Burns Federation which promotes education about Scotland and that fellowship of humanity which was one of Burns' major themes.

Representatives of both sides of a famous Scottish feud between the Campbells and MacDonalds attended this gathering. They referred a little nervously to the massacre at Glencoe, but didn't come to blows. Three hundred years after the fact, though, it still hovers in the background: a third party didn't want to admit which side of the feud her family was on.

There were even three men in kilts -- red Robertson, ancient Campbell, and the special tartan of the pipe band. I do love the swashbuckling swish of a kilt. Anyone who thinks they don't look masculine only has to look at the hairy legs emerging below, and the challenging look in the eye above, to be quickly set right.

This was a fine, nostalgic, Scots evening. You see? The best-laid plans o' mice and men don't always gang agley.

20

Here's a Northampton trivia question for you. You've probably heard that there's "only one" Main Street store that has only one storey. That's not quite right, though. Yup, there's another one. Give up?

If you haven't lived here long, you may never have noticed the tiny little shop called "Greetings" that's tucked between Faces and the building to the west which has seen a variety of shops come and go.

Greetings was started way back in 1948 by John and Gladys Hurley, in the building next door. When a larger store took over that building, they had to move up Main Street toward Edwards Church; but they missed their old location and were always looking for a way to get back to the center of town.

John Hurley, son of a former Fire Chief and a firefighter himself since 1945 (he later became Deputy Fire Chief) was doing some inspections on the roofs of Main Street one day. Just by chance he looked over the edge of the building where Faces now is, and saw a little strip of an alley which wasn't even visible from the street.

Aha, said he. Just the place. He talked with Joe Danziger, who owned it, and they worked out the details. A floor at street level and a roof above was about all it took -- plus an entry onto Main Street.

Greetings has been there ever since, and it's still only one storey.

When my husband Alec was approaching retirement, he started coming home with downtown scuttlebutt about which stores were going out of business or were for sale. We actually looked at Todd's, but it -- and all the others Alec mentioned -- were so big I was scared to even think about coping. But it began to sink in that Alec would like to buy a store. With what, I asked. A bank loan. Okay. Maybe.

Then one day he came home with the news that Greetings was up for sale. Now there was a store I had never even heard of. In fact, when I tried to find it to check it out, I walked right by it, twice.

When I finally did find my way in, I decided this was more my size. Alec was delighted, and we bought the business in 1969, the day Nixon became president.

We had a lot to learn about managing a store, in spite of Alec's business experience in running **WHMP**. Still, the Hurleys showed us the ropes, and taught us some age-old precepts like "Carry the entire line" and "You can't sell from an empty wagon."

Greetings was no empty wagon. Besides the sales floor, which was stuffed with merchandise up to the ceiling, the cellar below was crammed full, and had some gadgets like bowmakers, imprinters, and repair kits that were great fun to work with.

We soon found that both John and Gladys had an acute sense of humor. Our month learning the business was made not only pleasant, but fun, by their knowledge, good sense, cheerfulness, and shared laughter.

Then they left for a long-awaited vacation in Florida. We were still very green, and they promised to continue to advise us when they came back.

They never came back. Down in South Carolina, on their return trip, a 17-year-old in a hurry hit the curb and his car bounced across the highway into the Hurley's car. The teenager, John Hurley, and two friends who were with them, were killed instantly. Gladys was hospitalized for several days.

Family and friends went down to be with her when she regained consciousness. At first she seemed to be improving, but then one day she took someone's hand and drew a "J" in it. Was John...? Overcome, the family member couldn't answer. But that in itself was an answer. Gladys stopped fighting.

All of Northampton was in shock. They were a popular couple, and John, who was especially active in civic affairs, had such an exuberant zest for life that it didn't seem possible he was so suddenly gone.

Their friends would come in to Greetings looking stricken. Not to buy anything, but just to talk, to look around and remember. And the day of the funeral, most of Main Street closed down and moved up to St. Mary's Church. It was a long time before business seemed normal again.

There was a reason I mentioned Nixon taking office the day we bought Greetings. By a quirk of fate, the day we sold Greetings, Nixon resigned. We should have sold it earlier.

The shop has changed hands several times since then, gone into different lines of merchandise, been redecorated, put up more visible signs. But it still reminds many oldtime Northamptonites of a well-loved couple and of the incomprehensibility of fate.

21

Back when my husband and I bought Greetings, I was delighted to find among our business neighbors someone else with Maine connections.

Libby Whalen, at Whalen Stationers, had a Down East accent and the forthrightness and humor that go with it. To talk with her was to step back into my Maine childhood, to be splashed by the salt spray and join the clambake. I could even be heard to say "Ayuh" again.

Best of all, on those days when I was climbing the walls and needing to get away from the store, Libby could usually be counted on to be equally ready to play hookey and go get a cup of coffee at the old Woolworth's. A little letting off steam, a few laughs, and we would both be more willing to get back to the grind.

When we both left Main Street, we lost touch. She and her husband moved back to Maine -- at least for the summers -- and of course Alec and I went to Scotland.

Apparently the Whalens still see an occasional Gazette, because out of the blue came a note from Libby the other day, making one of those connections that I find so appealing. She sent me a clipping from the *Bangor Daily News*, showing a commencement speaker doing a handstand up near the ceiling, on top of a pile of chairs.

It was at my old high school, Gould Academy, the

one where Dick Dysart of the television show *L.A. Law* and I were classmates.

It seems the headmaster was getting pretty tired of the old cliche-ridden commencement speeches (as no doubt most headmasters do), and started looking around for someone who would give a silent "speech" instead.

He found Sam Kilbourn, a professional clown and part-time assistant attorney general -- an interesting combination -- who acted out a theme of personal challenge, risk-taking, and self-esteem. His costume for the occasion was not the usual pantaloons, frilly collar and red nose, just a simple cap and gown.

The event was not totally speechless. Kilbourn opened with a talk that must have jolted the listeners -- some long words thrown together with a dash of gibberish, to show the graduating class what they were missing.

From then on it was 15 minutes of "live interactive theater," with mime, slides, theatrical images and stage props -- what he and the group he works with call "new vaudeville" -- culminating in the spectacular handstand on his tower of chairs, from which he unfurled a banner that read "The Beginning."

I must say the old school sounds a bit different from when Dysart and I were there.

Or maybe not. The photo also shows some faces of the 1990 graduates in the audience, with the puzzled smiles of preppies who have just finished four years of serious exams and are wondering uneasily what they'll say if they're quizzed on this speech. They haven't caught on yet that from here on in, the questions don't come with answers.

Fortunately for them, only the class valedictorian got quizzed by the reporter present. What did he think of it? "It kept us on our toes."

I don't mean to poke fun at graduates, but

obviously the cliches are not only on the speaker's side of the podium.

Meantime, I have a bone to pick with Libby. She wrote, "This item reminded me of you. There are still clowns at Gould."

Still? Now what did she mean by that?

22

Every time I drive down State Street and see the old trolley tracks from the long-defunct Northampton Street Railway Companyre-emerging from under the asphalt, I smile to myself and decide to start off a column with them.

I was once a great trolley fan. When I was about 12 my family lived in Boston, near Cleveland Circle, where one of the Boston subway lines ended. Traveling frequently on that line, I got to know two or three of the drivers, who began to let me turn the lever to open the doors, just for the fun of it.

The next thing they let me do was cranking up the old coin machines. I'm not sure what that accomplished, actually -- perhaps it counted the coins. Some of the drivers would even let me clang the bell at street crossings.

I began to feel a bit like a subway mascot, and grew a little bolder, asking even drivers I'd never seen before if I could stand up front and watch. By then I knew a couple of drivers' names, and that was an open sesame.

My brother, who is four years older, used to make notes about the line, especially down in the subway in Boston proper, and learned how to keep going all over town on only one fare. The only trouble was he had to stay underground.

In all but Copley station, you could cross over to the other side, and in Park Street station you could even cross to another platform by zooming through the two open doors of a waiting car. Too bad if the doors closed before you got out. I've seen a few pigeons birdnapped that way.

Mapping out the stations served me well once in Paris, if I can digress a little. A Dutch friend and I had just got off a car in the Metro when the Hollander realized he'd left his briefcase aboard. He leaped back in, but then the doors closed. He was unfamiliar with Paris and looked aghast at getting separated from me this way. I took a quick look at the map behind me and then signalled to him to get off at the second stop, not the first. He nodded, and the train pulled out.

I dashed over to another line that also went to that second stop, and in fact arrived before the Dutch boy did, to his utter amazement! But back to Boston.

Before long, I was getting free rides to the end of the line and back -- to Lechmere, over an elevated section of the railway, and across a bridge. I was ecstatic at being in this position of privilege, allowed to open and shut the doors, crank up the coins, clang the bell, and watch the driver.

The final heights came when my particular driver-friend Andy Anderson asked if I'd like to drive the car, after the last passenger had left, around the long curve at the end of the line and into the car-barns. Naturally I said yes. What a treat to finally be at the helm of the streetcar -- one up on Judy Garland (who, if you've forgotten, sang "The Trolley Song" in "Meet Me in St. Louis." But she didn't drive it.)

Alas, after letting me do this several times, Andy joined the Seabees and went off to the Pacific, from which he sent me a few postcards. We moved shortly afterwards, and it was never the same again.

I didn't take up trolley driving as a career, although who knows, perhaps that's where I belonged.

Still, it ended up serving me in good stead as a writer. Several years ago I sold the story of my subway years to the Boston Globe, and they even started the story on page one.

Is it any wonder that when I see those brave remaining bits of track on State Street, I get a fit of nostalgia?

23

When you think about it, Northampton has a rare position in this country. How many cities or towns have been home to a president of the United States? I never really gave it much thought until I took my brother to FitzWilly's recently and mentioned that Cal Coolidge's old law office was just upstairs.

He gave me an unbelieving look, like the time I told him tobacco was a big crop here in happy valley. But once I had convinced him, he began to look suitably impressed.

Up until 1991, at least, the name of Calvin Coolidge was still painted on an inner door where now the firm of Grife, Walaszek & Ksieniewicz carries on in the same tradition of practicing law.

I have to admit I didn't have much interest in Coolidge until some years ago when I was given a copy of "The Talkative President" by Howard Quint and Robert Ferrell (UMass Press) to review for the Gazette.

Although Coolidge himself quoted a British reviewer "-- supposed to be a great authority -- who said he never read a book before he reviewed it because it might prejudice him," I not only read it but began to appreciate his dry wit.

For instance, on recurring reports that his Secretary of War had resigned: "The Secretary of War has not resigned. I don't expect he is going to resign, and I hope that for the sake of his peace of

mind that his resignation will not be reported in the
future oftener than once in two weeks."

Or early on the night of his imminent election,
when asked what states he expected to win: "I haven't
any specific reports about any states. My reports
indicate that I shall probably carry Northampton.
That is about as far as I can go into details."

Or, when asked if he was likely to say anything
while attending a fair the next day: "No, I am just
going as an exhibit."

When acknowledging that there might be differing
opinions about people in politics, he said, "I know
that, because I was Mayor of Northampton (1911-1914)
and after I had given a very excellent administration
for a year there was a division of opinion as to
whether I ought to be re-elected."

The information for much of the "Talkative
President" came from a wooden box that turned up at
the Forbes Library Coolidge collection in the 1960's,
some 30 years after Coolidge died. The box contained
the varbatim transcripts of all Coolidge's press conferences.

Silent Cal, said the authors in the introduction, had a reputation as "a small-boned, silent
Yankee politician propelled into the White House by
the accident of his predecessor's death and kept
there by the delusion of American voters in the
twenties."

The press conferences changed that image into
one of a "shrewd politician who demonstrated a surprisingly wide comprehension of public issues."

Will Rogers, who poked fun at presidents from
Teddy Roosevelt to Franklin Roosevelt, didn't leave
out Cal Coolidge. "He kept his mouth shut. That was
such a novelty among politicians that it just swept
the country."

Or, "President Coolidge gave a luncheon for

visiting governors where they discussed, but didn't try, prohibition."

Coolidge is scarcely considered one of our most outstanding presidents. He himself said that "Perhaps one of the most important accomplishments of my administration has been minding my own business," not a very impressive summing up of six years as head of state.

But at least he may have been the most famous mayor of Northampton. So far.

24

When I was a child in Maine and Boston, I often heard people tell my mother, "You look like Amelia Earhart."

I suppose it's possible that young people nowadays have never heard of Amelia, the first woman to fly across the Atlantic, the darling of America for her courage and tenacious spirit, a woman mourned by the whole nation when her plane was downed in the Pacific in 1937 on the last leg of an around-the-world flight.

Newcomers to this area may not be aware (although oldtimers surely are) that Amelia spent a little time here in Northampton in 1918, staying with her sister in an apartment on Bedford Terrace, to recuperate from an attack of pneumonia. Her sister Muriel was studying for the entrance exams to get into Smith, and the two sisters took many long walks in the area, up Mt. Tom, up the river towards Hatfield, and around Paradise Pond.

A local man, John Charlebois, was offering a five-week course in automobile mechanics for women. Here was a man ahead of his time! Amelia signed up for the course and by all accounts enjoyed herself.

In a letter she wrote to Charlebois in 1929 from the Cosmopolitan Magazine in New York City, where she was then aviation editor, she said:

"Thank you very much for sending me the picture of the Class of '18. Indeed I remember my work with you. It has stood me in good stead since, for it was a stepping stone for more thorough investigation of motors.

"Government requirements for securing transport licenses are becoming more severe as time goes on, and mechanical knowledge of the power plant is essential to pass the examination.

"I hope you have not discontinued your classes for I am sure there are many more girls today than ten years ago who wish to investigate 'what makes the wheels go round.'"

A copy of the letter, the aforementioned photograph of the "Class of '18," and a smiling picture of Amelia are still on display at the Tire Infirmary on Walnut Street, where the whine of electric wrenches and the clanging of tire irons resounds pleasantly on the sleepy street. Charlebois has retired, but Mike Chudy continues the business he bought a couple of years ago from its founder.

From time to time some new theory pops up about what happened to Amelia. Did she go down at sea? Or was she the mysterious white woman with amnesia who "came from the sky" and lived on a remote Pacific island? Was she interned in a Japanese prison camp? Was she buried on Saipan?

When word spread around the world that she was missing, US naval ships and aircraft, as well as chartered boats, criss-crossed 220,000 square miles of ocean, investigating thousands of islands and tiny atolls, but found no trace of Amelia and her navigator, Fred Noonan.

The aircraft carrier "Lexington," which had led the search, returned to San Francisco after two weeks, lowering the flag to half mast in honor of the lost flyers as she steamed under the Golden Gate bridge.

For years afterwards, alleged sightings, psychic visions, and downright hoaxes brought Amelia's name back to the headlines. The nation didn't want to let her go. But by now there are probably very few people who believe that Amelia will some day come winging her way back out of the sky.

I had nearly forgotten her myself when I moved out to Northampton from Boston, quite a few years ago now. But soon after arriving I was in Stop and Shop one day when a man who had been staring at me came over. "Did anyone ever tell you you look like Amelia Earhart?" he said.

My eyes smarted with sudden tears.

25

If life-experience is one of the main things that makes us different from each other, then experience with our cars has helped shape that difference.

For instance, there was the van I bought to move out to the Valley with. It stalled half-way up Mt. Sugarloaf, with my two-year-old in the front seat beside me and the baby sleeping way in the back, out of reach.

The emergency brake wouldn't hold while I tried to restart the van. Aha, I thought, I'll just back up against the fence. Wrong! The fence started to give way, too. So I sat there cliff-hanging, hoping no-one would come zooming up or down the hair-pin turns and crash into us, while I waited 20 minutes for the car to unflood. All the while chatting cheerfully to my two-year-old so he wouldn't be as terrified as I was.

That affected the way I view vans and Mt. Sugarloaf, if nothing else.

Then there was the station wagon that had vapor-lockitis. Whenever it got hot, it would just cut out, often at very inconvenient locations such as on bridges, turnpike entrance ramps, or mid-crossroads.

I kept a gallon jug of water in the car, and I'd hop out and pour it over the fuel pump. I got some very strange looks, but it worked.

I've had a car with rotten brakes, in which I made the kids sit on the floor in the back; one in which field mice filled up the air filter with bird-seed; one that caught fire -- luckily in the middle of a downpour; one where you had to move the spare tire to get at the dipstick.

There was the one AAA refused to come for any more -- it outwore their patience as well as mine.

There was the Renault I sold my brother. "Never sell a car to a relative," my husband said ominously, and he was so right. The car that had worked fine for me, wouldn't pass inspection in my brother's state, and cost him a lot of money. And although I'd sold it for less than I could have gotten elsewhere, I still paid him some money back. Never again, no matter how they beg!

Two of my three sons have crashed up my car, without damage to themselves. I'm not sure I want the third one to get a chance at it. But the youngest son said "it wasn't my fault" and went his merry way. The middle one took care of the insurance, paid the deductible, loaned me his own car, didn't spoil my vacation by telling me about it, and met me at the airport. Not that I'm making comparisons, or anything.

We had a car once that lost its ability to tell us how fast we were going. That's all right. We knew that when the car hit 60, it began to vibrate. When it was going 50, the roof rack hummed. At 40, the glove compartment fell open, and at 30 the cat pulled her head in from the window. We never did get that speedometer fixed.

We had a big station wagon when my youngest was small. On many trips to Florida he slept on a mattress in the back, and he was as much at home in that car as in our house. When we sold it, he cried.

It's no news that we get attached to our cars. After all, we spend rather a lot of time in them.

But it isn't just the fancy sports jobs or the brand new models that we get attached to. We get nostalgia kicks from the lemons and the clunkers, too.

They provide us with many a memory. In some inner part of us, those cars have made their dent on our lives, if I may use that word. Funny to think we would be altogether different if we hadn't had those particular cars, with all their idiosyncracies, teaching us aggressiveness, stress-handling, and basic mechanics.

Now I own a VW Rabbit. Why it has that name is a mystery. If mine is a rabbit, it must have been the one that lost the race with the tortoise. I think it's teaching me patience. Again.

26

Have you ever noticed that field over in Hadley, just off Route 9 between Frank's and the veterinary center, that seems to be growing a crop of forlorn, crooked posts?

Some of you will no doubt remember what those posts are -- the last remnants of the former Hadley Drive-in movie theater.

Do you sometimes wonder if there are any drive-in movies still around? Most of them vanished in those years when good movies simply weren't being made, and television held everyone at home, nose to tube.

There's little reason to suppose drive-ins will ever return. Movies may be making a comeback, but the special uses of a drive-in have changed. If a family wants cheap entertainment, they can rent a video. And the hormone-filled teens who gave drive-ins the nickname of "passion pits" don't seem to need a date at the movies as an excuse any more.

As a child, I never got to go to one of these exciting, forbidden pleasure domes, but when we'd see one from the highway, like the one at Ogunquit, Maine, my brother and I would hang out the windows, enviously watching the soundless picture from the road as long as we could.

There's a whole generation of people by now who have never experienced one. How amazing! The one in Hadley was full nearly every night, the cars driving one by one onto their tiny lots. We would unhitch the loudspeaker from the post, enjoy the somewhat fresh air, talk in semi-privacy, and even if we ate the traditional popcorn, there was something about it that was more exciting, more fun than a regular movie theater.

The time when Hadley Drive-In -- and sometimes the Red Rock in Southampton -- became an important part of my life was when I became a single mother with two young kids. Money being as tight as it was, going to the movies and paying for a babysitter was just something I didn't do. But with a drive-in, I could get out of the house and take the kids along.

At the drive-in, or even before, I'd settle the kids to sleep on the back seat, and watch the movie in peace. I could take along a snack. I wouldn't get sneezed on by my neighbors. Yet there I was, out of the house, among other people, enjoying the latest film.

Sometimes there would be entertainment even before the movie started. Several people would use moveable spotlights to weave random patterns on the darkened screen. It could get to be rather beautiful, and sometimes amusing. A unique art form I've never seen anywhere else.

What finally put an end to our weekly jaunts was that movie about the sinking ocean liner. I had seen scary movies there before, but this one really had the adrenaline flowing. Right in the middle of the scene where the little girl is about to fall down a shaft, I heard a small noise and looked around. Instead of being asleep, both my boys were hanging bug-eyed over the back of the seat, watching.

I got them to lie down again, but as soon as my back was turned, they got up. They were as obedient as most children.

I tried coaxing. They weren't listening. I threatened to leave. I think they knew I wouldn't be able to. So eventually I got them into the front seat where I could at least put a comforting arm around them.

When the movie finally ended, all three of us were emotionally exhausted. I thought the kids would be asleep by the time we got home, but they were hyper instead, talking on and on about the movie.

I knew that once they realized I had been depriving them of something exciting, our drive-in days were over. They'd never sleep there again.

Nowadays people can stay at home and watch what they like, and a "drive-in" is a place that serves food instead of entertainment.

And all that's left of the drive-in movie is an occasional back lot full of abandoned posts, a forgotten field of dreams.

27

The '92 election has brought up memories of the 1948 election in which Harry Truman confounded all the experts who said he was going to lose, and won.

President Bush keeps bringing it up, for obvious reasons -- he too is an incumbent president who is doing poorly in the polls. This week's television showed Truman's campaign, too, and his victory speech in which Ronald Reagan was his right-hand man, speaking for a rather different party than the one he ended up with.

I have my own memories of that campaign, although I was not very politically aware in those days. Was it fate, I wonder, that made my path cross Harry Truman's? I didn't even know he was in town, and I'm pretty sure he didn't know I was, either.

It was late October, just a few days before the election, as now. I was a freshman at Boston University, and on October 27 I was running late. It was my mother's birthday and I had meant to bake her a cake, but being a haphazard person in my younger days, I hadn't gotten around to it.

My last class was physical education, and to save time, I left my blue gym suit, with its short skirt and voluminous bloomers, on under my other clothes. I dashed out, grabbed my bike and headed home to 27 Marlborough Street.

I had, at least, bought a cake mix, but when I got home and picked it up, I realized that I had no eggs and that it would never be done in time for dinner. The only alternative was to run over to a bakery on Tremont Street and pick one up.

It was nearly the five-o'clock rush hour as I charged across the public gardens and crossed busy Tremont Street. But the bakery was still open, and even had a cake with "Happy Birthday" already iced on it. They added "Mom," I counted out the pay, and happily went back out onto the street.

But things had changed dramatically in the half hour or so since I had entered the shop. Instead of quickly-moving pedestrians, I came up against a solid wall of onlookers. Peering through gaps in the crowd, I could see that the usual bumper crop of cars had been exchanged for a slowly-moving cavalcade, complete with mounted policemen, cheers and general commotion.

Dismayed, I wondered how I was going to get across the street and home with the cake before my mother turned up. I was so intent on my own agenda, I didn't even wonder what the parade was all about.

I weaseled my way to the edge of the curb, and looked up the street. Perhaps if I went up further, I could go around the parade.

Then, as I hesitated, a gap opened up in the motorcade. The next car was at some distance up Tremont Street. Although the police were holding the crowds to the sidewalk, nobody was looking at me. Did I dare chance it? You guessed it. I was getting desperate.

I darted into the street, and promptly tripped and fell. I managed to maneuver the cake box so that it fell upright, but then, the breath knocked out of me, I stayed where I was and began to laugh.

What a picture I had to make, with my gym bloomers sticking up in the air and my nose in the dirt. I giggled helplessly, not eager to get up and face the crowds, nor the police, for that matter.

After a moment, a man in a Brooks Brothers suit and topcoat, looking every inch the proper Bostonian, helped me to my feet.

That's when I looked up and saw that the on-coming car had stopped. Sitting on the back seat of the convertible was President Truman, with Mayor Curley and ex-governor Paul Dever. Two secret service men had their guns drawn, and one of them was pointed at me.

Gulping a little, I grinned reassuringly up at them and ran a hand through my unruly hair.

The secret service men relaxed, and the president smiled and waved at me. I picked up my cake and, with more bravado than good sense, kept going across the street. The crowd on the other side smilingly opened up for me, and I sped on home, every now and then spilling another giggle onto the sidewalk, disconcerting the pigeons and other passersby.

The cake wasn't badly damaged. As I recall, my mother liked it. As for me, I was just thankful that neither the cake nor I had been aerated by bullet holes.

I was not sorry that our paths never crossed again.

28

If there's one thing I do fairly well, it's run out of gas. It happens about once a year, and although I tear my hair and cry "Why, why?", deep in my heart I know why. It's stupidity.

So last Thursday I noticed the gas gauge was getting low, and thought I should refill sometime soon. And Friday I merrily set off on the 75-mile trip to Bradley Airport to pick up a friend.

We were on the way back, somewhere in Springfield, when the engine gave that polite little hiccup I've learned to recognize. Hastily but carefully I crossed two lanes of traffic to ease into the breakdown lane before the car rolled to a stop.

After kicking myself mentally for a few minutes, I got out in the cold to try to look helpless. This may have worked 20 years ago, but I'm a little too hefty for helpless now. So after a few minutes of stomping around, I told Martha I was going to walk back to the entrance ramp we had just passed, to see if there were any service stations near by.

As I got to the ramp, down which it looked pretty residential, a car even older than mine drove up it, and I tentatively put out my hand. The car stopped, and I explained my predicament to the driver, a man in his 40s. Could he at least take me to the next exit, where there might be more gas stations? Because my car takes diesel, and diesel is very hard to find.

Sure, hop in, he was going that way anyway, on his way to the store. As we passed the car, I waved at Martha, and thought she waved back, but in fact she didn't see me, as I learned later.

The driver, Ramon, took me to the nearest gas station, which naturally did not have diesel, but they gave us directions to one that did. I hesitantly asked Ramon if he could drive me there. Sure. We set off, but must have missed a turning, because we never found it. We stopped at another gas station and got directions to another diesel source. Would Ramon drive me there as well? Sure.

By this time I was thoroughly lost, but not Ramon. In fact, we were just passing his house, where his wife and two daughters would no doubt have been surprised if they were looking out the window at the time. They had all come up from Puerto Rico only four years ago.

We stopped at a couple of other stations, just in case, but diesel was not on their menu. Finally we arrived at the diesel station -- and there were no containers I could use to take it back to my car. I couldn't believe it, but the man was adamant. So it was back to Ramon. How long would he stick with this? Would he drive me up to Springfield Plaza so I could buy a container? Sure. By this time we were both laughing at this wild goose chase.

I bought the container (which will now remain in my car) and we started off again. We cruised in and out of five stations, then got back on 91 and off at the next exit, where miraculously there was a station with diesel. At last.

Back to 91 again, and I wondered aloud whether the police were about to tow my car away, Martha or no Martha. Sure enough, there was a police car, about to call in the tow truck. And there was Martha, who thought I had vanished for good.

Ramon poured in the diesel as I praised him to the skies for being such a good Samaritan. There are still good people in this world; friendly, helpful people who will go out of their way for us idiots. Vaya con dios, amigo.

Perhaps that's why I keep running out of gas: to keep on testing the real world of good people, instead of learning to believe the TV world of baddies.

Hey, I like that explanation better than the "stupidity" one.

29

I haven't been to UMass Fine Arts Center events for a while, and had forgotten what a high standard they have. But after two shows there in the past two weeks, I have to say who needs New York?

"Fiddler on the Roof" was playing there on September 20th in a revival of the 1964 musical by the Troika Organization in association with Music Theatre Associates, Inc.

I've loved this show since before it happened. Back when I was at Boston University, my English professor, Donald Born, had a weekly radio program on which he read stories. I remember listening, fascinated, as he read Scholem Aleichem's "Reb Tevye and his Daughters." Of course I never pictured it as a musical, but luckily someone else did.

Later I got to know Sol Jacobson, who reputedly was one of those instrumental in getting the Fiddler to Broadway. I never heard the details, but it gave me a proprietary feeling toward the show, as if I hadn't had one already.

After the show last week, actor Marty Ross was telling us that when Fiddler opened in Japan, critics wondered how it could be popular in Europe, when it was so obviously Japanese.

And watching it again at UMass I was struck anew, myself, with how brilliantly this Russian-Jewish character of Reb Tevye represents Everyman, with his security blanket of "Tradition" battling with his warm heart and generous nature; with his dreams of "If I Were a Rich Man" becoming ridiculous as he plans absurd ways to spend his money -- one staircase going up, one coming down, and one going nowhere, "just for show." With his light-hearted arguments with God, even as he sees the futility of what he's asking.

There's just a hint of contrivance in the fact that the daughters marry such a rainbow of husbands -- the radical sent to Siberia, the childhood friend, the non-Jewish Russian -- despite the efforts of the matchmaker to marry them off to more traditional choices.

If the humor is delicious, the music is poignant. "Sunrise, Sunset" is the cri de coeur of every parent who wonders "how did they suddenly grow up?" And "Anatevka" strikes a chord with everyone who has left a beloved home behind.

The choreography was brilliant, particularly in the dream scene where a gigantic ghost and a swirl of colorful relatives sway like underwater anemones in a storm.

I had never really understood the reference to a "Fiddler on the Roof," but Ross, who played the basso Lazar the Butcher, made it a little clearer by desribing a painting of the same name by Marc Chagall, himself of Russian-Jewish origin. The dwarfish violinist perched on the ridgepole represents the precariousness of life, teetering on the edge of poverty, persecution, and dispersion. But it also represents the will to rise above it, to get on with life, to dance in the face of disaster.

There were several scenes that were especially striking -- the Sabbath prayer scene, the wedding, and the lonely railroad station.

When "Fiddler on the Roof" opened, many thought it was a big gamble. Who would be interested in a Jewish farmer living in a tiny Russian village? They needn't have worried. This show will be returning again and again, warming each new generation and making us question our prejudices.

Another group that has lived with prejudice, poverty, and exile, with a fiddler teetering on the roof -- but this time in our own country -- are the American Indians. Wednesday night it was their turn to be on stage at UMass, and a spectacular show it was.

A number of Indian tribes were represented in the cast and in the dances, and although the differences were apparent, so too was the basic rootedness in the land which is common to them all.

The dancing is not what our own culture is used to. You don't find precision dancing or jazzy choreography here. What you do find, if you look long and deeply enough, is an integrity that carries its own power.

The Eagle Dance, with a winged troupe soaring in the clouds as "messengers between man and the Creator" was a particular favorite.

Gorgeous, authentic costumes, some handed down from generation to generation; haunting flute melodies; an acrobatic hoop dance that was received with great enthusiasm by the audience; excellent lighting; hypnotic drums, and a grand finale that showed American Indian dress in all its true glory -- this was an evening that was distinctly different, yet with its own poignancy and majesty.

Bravo to UMass! And guess who's coming to dinner there on Monday?

30

I'm as escapist as the next person. Give me too much murder and mayhem on TV and I'll start watching Cosby reruns. Give me a little too much Civil War gore and I'll start reading Thurber. Talk about war in the Middle East and I'll sign up for a course in comedy writing at UMass.

I figured that even if I never learned to write comedy, it should be a fun class -- and it was.

There was Alan, who after four classes debuted at the "open mike" at the Iron Horse. He seems destined for the borscht circuit. Then there was Michael, an emigre from the USSR, who has a bumper sticker in Russian, translating as "no problem." He probably indeed won't have a problem becoming a comic.

Norma sat in the corner for five weeks, pretending mousedom, and then on the last day threw off her disguise and had us in stitches. Susie's housewifely take-off on Hamlet's soliloquy broke us up; the engineer in the back row warmed up gradually over the weeks until he was quite human; the businessman wanted to learn how to "roast" people. It seemed incongruous -- his friendly, kindly face was as far from Don Rickles as you can get.

And of course there was our instructor, Izzy Gesell, who is not only a pro, but has heart, too.

I sort of hate to admit that I've taken the course, in case my readers are disappointed that I don't suddenly become amusing. I've always admired

people who could write funny stuff, but have never
had the illusion that I was talented in that direc-
tion. So hey, don't blame me -- after all, the
course was only five weeks long. If it had been six
weeks it might have been different.

We certainly need humor in our lives, and the
worse things get, the more we need it. Now that
we're officially in a recession, comedians should
become even more popular -- so if you know any
comics, make friends with them now, before they move
up in the world.

Of course Oscar Wilde thought humor could have
its drawbacks: "Nothing spoils a romance so much as a
sense of humor in the woman."

On the other hand, some authors have given a
sense of humor very high marks, even saying it gives
us patience for "the vicissitudes of human exist-
ence." (Richard Monckton Milnes, no relation.)

If it's that useful, perhaps we ought to make it
a requirement of our politicians. Surely we could do
without leaders who take themselves too seriously.
Though I suppose politicians do have a good laugh now
and then -- on us.

We could even have humor courses in the Pentagon. After all, the language of humor is often
lethal: "I died laughing," "she kills me," or "he
bombed in Vegas." Wonder if in some future generation someone will win a war by making his enemy
helpless with laughter? If the government wants to
give me a grant, I'll be glad to study the possibili-
ties.

Norman Cousins, on the other hand, claims
laughing is healing rather than "killing." Either
way, it's likely to stay around a while. Sometimes
it's the only thing that gets us through the day.

In spite of rattling sabers, drug wars, homelessness and numerous other vicissitudes, life is
pretty comic. In fact, one of the ways to teach humor

writing is simply to get us to observe the life around us.

Who can, or needs to, make up anything funnier than that?

31

There's a box of my youngest son's school papers sitting in my closet, waiting for me to go through them before they're thrown out. A few tests labeled "A" -- precious because so few and far between; some special projects, neatly bound; and a large variety of drawings.

I've always been fascinated by children's drawings. They're in a different category from the paintings of masters, but in many cases, I like the kid stuff better.

Not being much of an artist myself, I used to wonder how it was that almost any kid would take up a paintbrush without self-consciousness, and paint a picture that he or she was proud to bring home to mom.

When we lived on Massasoit Street, my oldest son even did a creditable oil painting, at age five, in the studio of our neighbor, Jim Waldron.

When my youngest was at Cloverdale Nursery School at St. John's Episcopal Church, one of my favorite pastimes as the "helping mother" was to watch the kids paint.

After a while I think I figured it out. It wasn't that they were all talented, but that they were willing to change when necessary. Adults, or at least myself, are too judgmental about what we draw. If it doesn't look like we think it should, we throw it out and give it up.

But kids were instantly adaptable. If the paint started running down the paper, the kid's concept of what he was painting instantly changed, and he or she would accommodate the "mistake" into something new and possibly better.

My fascination with children's art even shows up in my collection of odds and ends from my Gazette-reporter days. One of my "beats" was the schools, and I used to go around visiting them in turn, getting a story on some project that was happening at each school. It might be a science fair, a field trip, a play or concert, or some hilarious recipes for Thanksgiving stuffing (like lettuce and peanut butter); but very often, it would be art. Amazingly good art.

One of my souvenirs from those days, 25 years ago, is a picture page on a "show and tell" in Miss Grace's kindergarten class at Jackson Street School, an event which would probably be very similar to one today. A raccoon tail, pictures of birds, a jump-rope, pussywillows, a German Army hat, and a spider were all equally appreciated by the teacher, or at least she graciously said so.

One boy forgot what you called the binoculars he brought in, but demonstrated how they "shrimp and grow." A pair of twins had made a book, stapled together by their father, "but he put in one page upside down."

Some of the kids on that picture page are undoubtedly parents themselves now. Will they recognize the reappearance of the cycle when their kids ask "what can I take for show and tell," or bring home those colorful drawings?

The more things change, the more they stay the same. Year after year kids go to kindergarten, make their pictures, and bring them home to be displayed (at least for a while) on the refrigerator door. I went through all that with three kids; now I have drawings from three grandchildren on my walls.

Strangely enough, the cycle may repeat itself, but those pictures are all different, as unique as a fingerprint. At kindergarten age we are already individuals with unique gifts to offer the world.

That box of my son's drawings? Guess I'll keep them after all.

32

Local author Tracy Kidder has been "Among Schoolchildren" and written a fine book about Holyoke teacher Chris Sajak and her class.   Some of the rest of us may have been among schoolchildren, too, but never had the courage to be truthful about what went on.

As Kidder points out, it's a lonely business. And don't let anyone tell you it's easy.

I taught for a while. Sometimes to adults, as at the Berlitz School of Languages in Paris, and at a training session for Peace Corps volunteers at UMass.

I've also taught on the high school level: two years at Northampton School for Girls (now merged with Williston Academy), and a very short stint as a substitute teacher in the Northampton public school system.

I didn't take very happily to teaching. I did it in Paris because there were few other jobs open to a foreigner, but I was pushing myself, and I knew it. Somehow I thought teaching kids would be easier.

At NSFG I enjoyed the kids. I enjoyed planning the lessons. I didn't even mind correcting the endless homework. The classes were small -- eight to ten girls -- and the pay wasn't bad. I even got some positive feedback about my teaching.

But every weekend I felt relief. Every vacation week was bliss. The coming of summer was like a weight off my back. Why would I want to do it a second year? I decided that one year wasn't giving it enough of a chance, that's why. Maybe the second year would be better.

It wasn't, it was worse. Planning lessons all over again wasn't fun any more. I had a couple of discipline problems, more so than the first year, and I wasn't good at handling them. I admire enormously teachers who can.

After the second year I thankfully bowed out, convinced that this was not the job for me.

Many years later, after returning to this area, I began to feel the need for more income and wondered if I would be considered too over the hill to get a job. If you're ever in this position, take heart: I applied for four part-time jobs, and got them all.

One was as a substitute teacher, and I got a call right away to teach French at the High School. At least I thought it was just French until I got there; then I found out one class was Spanish. Though I'd had two years of it and had visited Spain and Mexico, I couldn't have felt rustier.

But luck was with me. A student teacher took the first French class, while I boned up on the Spanish lesson in the back of the room. Nothing like being just one step ahead.

My son James, a fairly recent graduate of NHS at the time, had warned me. "Mom," he said, "don't be a sub, they'll bury you." Pooh, I thought. It can't be that bad.

Well, to be honest, it wasn't great. I'd been told that kids would give the wrong name, that they'd be rowdy, that they'd talk to each other and ignore the teacher.

All this all happened, and more. On the way to lunch, something hit me in the side of the head. That, I admit, was off-putting. I looked around and saw nothing but innocent backs of heads. I never knew whether it was personal (after three hours?), accidental (no apology?), or generic. If the latter, it felt like war. How have we let relations between adults and kids deteriorate so badly?

I got a few more 7 a.m. calls, and managed to pluck up courage to say yes, I'd sub. But when they asked me one Monday to teach on Thursday, I had too many days to anticipate the fun I wouldn't be having. I still had two of my other part-time jobs. How many did I need? I called in and quit.

Over to you, Chris Zajac and company. With admiration and chagrin.

33

Of all the concentric and overlapping circles that make up a community, the circle that comes closest to the city's heart may well be made up of the local politicians.

The neighbors may see a new school going up; the teachers and students may become all too familiar with the interior. But it's the politicians who argued for it, worried about the finances, wrangled late into the night over the plans, shoveled the first earth, stood in the rain for the laying of the cornerstone, and whose names in the entryway are now seldom noticed -- it's they who have the spirit of that school in the palm of their hands.

They haven't just watched as their city took shape; they've been intimately involved.

I was just shown around Northampton England by one of its former mayors, Cyril Benton, and somewhere on Guildhall Street I suddenly realized that it has taken thousands of caring people, during its 800-year history, to shape it into the livable, prosperous, attractive place it now is.

One of those people was George Washington's great-grandfather, twice mayor of Northampton.

Our sister city has changed enormously since I last saw it in 1970, and it seems obvious that a number of people had to have vision and daring in order to make that a change for the better.

Cities do change. You grow up in a place and familiarity may make it seem static, but that's not possible. Boston, for instance, has improved since I lived there back in the '50s. Quincy Market, the spruced up subway system, the government complex that replaced Scollay Square -- there had to be interested, concerned people to make these improvements happen.

When we came back to 'Hamp after an absence of 10 years, we were pleased by the new bike path, the more usable Pulaski Park, the busy downtown that had made a comeback after being pronounced dead by the mall promoters. People here have been caring, too.

When you stop to think of it, there must be thousands of towns all over the world fortunate enough to have citizens who think about the future, about beautification and renewal and business and jobs, and work to make it all happen.

Often, those movers and planners are the local politicians, yet very few politicians are considered heroes.

They have to balance plans against finances; have to fight against footdragging, apathy, contrariness, miserliness; have to prop up the pros and pacify the cons. In the process, they make enemies. They are accused of hogging the spotlight, of being hypocrites and manipulators; in short, they are accused of being "politicians." But they get things done.

Even when my husband Alec was in local politics, I didn't really appreciate all he and his colleagues at City Hall accomplished, nor all they had to put up with, nor all the compromises they had to make.

Perhaps you have to see it afresh, in a different place. In our English namesake town, Cyril Benton was so eager to show me around, so pleased with what he and other Borough Councillors had achieved, and so forthright about what didn't please him at all, that I could see the whole machinery of politics through his eyes.

Cyril is at home all over his city; in the Guildhall (Town Hall) where he's long been a councillor; in Derngate, the exciting new entertainment center which Cyril helped bring into being; at new Swallow Inn, where he climbed on the roof to "top it off" in the dedication of the building; at the hospital, where he circulated during the kick-off reception for a "friends of the hospital" organization; at Market Square, where he sighed regretfully at the new paving which he had voted against; walking through the downtown area, where he stopped to talk with someone every few feet.

It's obvious that the politician, in spite of everything, gets very real satisfactions from being at the heart of things. It's a full, social, busy, productive life, which contributes not only to the present-day advancement of the community you live in, but also to its eventual history.

I hope, now that I've noticed, I'll be more appreciative of what our local politicians are getting done. And may there always be people who will be motivated to spend some of their time for the public good, in the democratic tradition of self-government that goes back, not just to 1776, but to far more ancient roots.

34

When some friends from Scotland came to visit me, they enjoyed visiting Mt. Tom, Smith College, and other local points of interest. But what do you suppose they asked to be shown? Diners.

That's right, diners. With cameras at the ready, I drove them to see the Bluebonnet, Miss Florence, the Red Lion. They were fascinated.

Growing up with diners part of the background, we don't realize that diners represent something uniquely American, something a foreigner might be intrigued by.

Richard J. S. Gutman, who wrote a book about diners, claims the diner didn't start as a railroad car but as a horse drawn lunch wagon, the first one debuting in Providence in 1872. But later, abandoned streetcars were transformed into diners, and these were often in such poor shape that the diner began to have a bad reputation.

The basic diner menu of the '50s was meatloaf, coffee and pie, with breakfast available all day. The pie was almost by definition mouth-watering. The coffee and meatloaf might vary from place to place. But recent diners, brought to life by an increasing interest in the tradition, may serve French wine and exotic dishes, and demand that you make reservations.

There were perhaps 6,000 diners across the U.S. in the 1950s, at the height of their popularity, says Gutman. With the rise of fancier restaurants, the number of diners dropped to about 2,200 before renewed interest in them saw a comeback to nearly their former numbers.

The image of the tough waitress blowing bubble gum and insulting the customers may or may not be part of the diner tradition, but if it was, the customers seemed to like it.

For me, the endearing and enduring part of diners is the community spirit they foster. Most of the customers are "regulars" and the conversation is usually more general than in a restaurant. Diner customers often banter back and forth in the cozier, more intimate ambiance, and look forward to their daily encounters.

The community spirit still lives in places like the former Red Lion diner on Pearl Street, whose owner became well-known for her friendliness and gener-osity, and for whom our local shelter, Jessie's House, was named.

Both during the depression years, when the diner was a source of moral support as well as of good and inexpensive food, and during the war years, when their quick service was appreciated by workers who had little time to relax, the diner was the eatery of choice for the everyday breakfast, quick lunch, or much-needed coffee break.

Part of the tradition of diners has been plenty of parking space, since the familiar railroad-car design attracted truckers like magnets. One of the pieces of folk wisdom in the 50s was that travelers should look for a diner surrounded by trucks, as a guarantee of good food.

When diners started wearing out, many were torn down or converted. Northampton is fortunate that the owners of Miss Florence, in the heart of Florence, and Bluebonnet on King Street, had the good sense to leave their original buildings intact, and simply added other facilities on at the back. Red

Lion, with the railroad at its back, had no place to expand, and simply remained as it was.

With the return of the diner to greater popularity, these originals are now seen as fascinating historical landmarks.

For many of us locals, though, they are too familiar to be noticed, until some visitor arrives from Britain and points them out to us with eager cries of joy.

35

I became a flag-waver the other day. It was a dark blue little flag with the famous photograph of our planet, taken from space. I bought it for $2 in the basement of Thornes, and decided to carry it home, right out in the open.

Just a few feet down Main Street someone stopped me to ask where I got it. (Maybe flagwaving is going to catch on.) Later, someone asked if the flag meant I had been in a peace demonstration downtown. I'm not sure why waving an Earth flag gives one a label - - can't I just love the planet I belong to?

It reminded me of the brouhaha twenty-five years or so ago, when then Mayor Wallace Puchalski took down off City Hall, where it had waved harmlessly for several years, the United Nations flag that a local women's group had donated to the city. The quarrel went on for some weeks, and finally the little blue flag went back up next to Old Glory.

It isn't there now, though, and wondering what had happened to 'it started me thinking about whether the United Nations flag is really what we need. Yes, the UN is a brave effort, bringing nations together to meet face to face. But it is also a collection of governments, rather than a collection of the people of Earth themselves. People seem able to get along together pretty well; it's governments that have wars.

That compelling photograph of our common planet, blue seas and orange land masses, swirled round with white cloud formations, gives a different picture than a world map with its man-made borders. Looking at the more-inclusive space photo, it's more obvious that we are all one species, and that it just doesn't make sense to try to blow up parts of our own home.

Nobody's borders are visible from space. Man has divided up the planet into puny kingdoms, sheikdoms, and national security states, but the universe pays no attention. Our planet is too small, and our weapons now too big, for borders to protect us. Chernobyl should have told us that if we didn't know it already.

Our best hope in this age of technology and nuclear capability is to decide that settling disputes through weaponry has become as old-fashioned as hand-to-hand combat on horse-back, wearing chain mail. As Roger Fisher of Harvard Law School pointed out, "There is no way that we can make our end of the boat safer by making the other end more likely to tip over."

It's too bad that our leaders still think in the old, worn-out terms of force and weapons, and that a primeval aggressiveness can so easily be called forth among otherwise peaceful Americans. Maybe life is so frustrating that it feels good to be able to lash out at an enemy, to rally around a common flag.

Mind you, I can understand the appeal of the Stars and Stripes. It can look very stirring, rippling out in the breeze, especially when you come across it unexpectedly in a foreign land. It's easy to get emotional about it.

But I was struck by something my son said when he came back here after several years in England. "The flags are so huge!" he said, wonderingly, and I looked around with new eyes and saw that yes, they were. They had grown bit by bit over the years, so slowly I hadn't noticed.

I'm sorry to say that I wondered whether there was a correlation somewhere, between bigger flags and lesser values. As our country's problems have grown worse, has the flag gotten bigger to gloss it over? Is it more of the "image instead of substance" philosophy of the Reagan era?

Sure, I love the American flag. It's beautiful, and it used to stand for something of value. I hope it still does. But we also have state flags, organization flags, welcome flags -- so there seems no harm in promoting a more inclusive Earth flag, too, to remind us all of our membership in the whole human race. That one, I don't mind waving on Main Street.

36

There's no sign on the Walnut Street estab-
lishment of Messrs. Czelusniak et Dugal, and if you
walked in out of curiosity you might be puzzled at
first by the stacks of oddly shaped wood full of
holes, the sheets of kangaroo skin, the metal pipes
of all sizes stacked in the corners.

What goes on here? Pipe organ tuning and
maintenance, that's what. An unusual business
indeed, with craftsmanship on many complex levels,
demanding a familiarity not only with wood, metal and
leather, but also with electricity. Low voltage DC
is used in many organs to transmit signals from the
keys to the pipes.

The staff of five or six obviously enjoy their
work. One man is working to music -- organ music, of
course -- from a cassette player. This is a job
there's no training for except on-the-job, and one
would have to love it to be here.

It began as a hobby for Bill Czelusniak of
Southampton. When he was starting high school a new
organ was installed in the family church in Easthampton, and it fired his imagination. A growing
fascination for pipe organs kept him learning about
the instrument through his years at Williston.

In 1970, when he began working toward a BA and
then an MA in marketing at UMass, he also began doing
part-time organ cleaning and maintenance work around

Northampton, teaming up with a business partner, Francis Dugal of Florence.

Coincidently, Dugal had similarly become interested in the organ at the local church during his own high school days in Hatfield a generation earlier.

By 1976 the two were working full-time and had contracts with Smith College, Amherst, and the University of Massachusetts for organ tuning and maintenance.

For many years they worked out of their respective homes. In 1989, when they needed to expand and bought the former Moore Business Systems building on Walnut Street, they didn't realize at first that their space had been dedicated to music once before. Back in 1886 this was the Hyde Violin Factory, where Andrew Hyde crafted stringed instruments.

According to his 1905 obituary, Hyde was "famous as an American maker of violins rivalling those of the old masters, a genius of rare mechanical talent." "Mechanical talent" seems an odd phrase for a violin-maker, but "violin factory" also sounds a bit quaint to 20th century ears.

Hyde was also noted for two ancient violins he owned: one made by Nicholas Amati in 1673, priced 100 years ago at $1,000, and one made by Andreas Guarnerni, who died in 1698 ($600). Those prices are a bit out of date.

The building went through several remodelings, and during World War II was expanded with government assistance to enable the machine shop there to specialize in brass shell casings. The progression isn't always swords into plowshares, sometimes it's shell casings into organ pipes.

Messrs. Czelusniak et Dugal were incorporated in 1978, and that same year they renovated the 1883 organ in the First Congregational Church in Adams, and then the circa 1875 organ in the Cummington village church.

The 19th century Westfield organ builders, Johnson & Son, had provided many of organs in this area (as well as further afield), and Czeluzniak and Dugal worked on an 1860 one at the Episcopal Church in Ashfield and an 1892 one in the Congregational Church in Monson, before tackling the larger project of removing an 1896 Johnson & Son organ, no longer in use, from Northampton State Hospital, cleaning and renovating it, and installing it at Holyoke Community College.

"Sometimes," Czelusniak notes, "moving an organ doesn't work out well. The room may be a different size or shape, for instance. But we've been lucky." When you think about it, organs aren't mass produced, but are built for a specific space.

Simply tuning an organ, with its multiplicity of pipes, might cost anywhere from $200 to $1,800. A modest overhaul could run in the neighborhood of $30,000, and a major rebuilding could go as high as $200,000.

Their latest project is work on the organ of the Skinner Memorial Chapel at the Second Congregational Church in Holyoke. The organ is spread out all over the Walnut Street premises at the moment, getting its many parts checked, cleaned, rebuilt where needed. As an example of the firm's meticulous attention to detail, Czelusniak and Dugal searched out a supplier in Ohio whose work most matched the orginal, and had them make the replacement casings.

A surprising number of parts are re-usable. Czelusniak can tell by the style of painting that some of the wooden pipes, still in excellent condition, predate 1921, and there are pipes down in the basement dating from Civil War times. The oldest known organ still in continuous use is one in Sion,

Switzerland, made in 1390. Organs don't seem to wear out as fast as people do.

Besides the poplar and pine woods used in pipes and casings, and the zinc and lead pipes which give a different tone from the wood, a number of animal hides are used for valves, gaskets, and "reservoirs" (a kind of bellows). Hides include horse, cow, sheep, and kangaroo skins, the latter imported from Australia under special regulations, and not always available. Each hide has different properties that make it useful for a particular part of the instrument.

An organ is a unique combination of the natural, such as the wood and leather, and the man-made, as in metal parts and electric key action. Of course there are fully electric organs as well, but it sometimes happens that a church may discard an electric organ in favor of a pipe organ. There just isn't the same fascination in an electronic gadget as there is in a majestic set of eight-foot wooden pipes with their deep, mournful tones.

The organ workers' vocabulary expands to include wind chests, chimney flutes, reed racks, flue pipes, miters, ear flaps, toe holes and goodness knows what else. It's a very small world of its own, but surprisingly there are perhaps 40 such firms in New England alone.

It's reassuring to know that in this technological age craftsmanship is not dead after all, but very much alive on Walnut Street.

37

Russ Flanagan, whose obituary notice appeared in the Gazette in January of '94, was a somewhat legendary figure in the Gazette office. He was the Easthampton correspondent, and his clear, apt, thorough stories on all aspects of life in his town clattered over the teletype every morning without fail for more than 30 years.

He was also legendary because we almost never saw him in person. I don't remember him ever dropping in at the Gazette offices, although he may have, and he didn't seem to come to Gazette parties, although he was invited. So he remained somewhat of a mystery man, a disembodied teletype writer like those anonymous beings at Associated Press.

Ed O'Dea, who was the managing editor in those days, spoke admiringly of the way Russ covered his territory, and gave him full credit for keeping competitors at bay. The late lamented Holyoke Transcript, a paper we all admired, made periodic efforts to take over Easthampton, but Russ -- I pictured him on horseback -- held them off at the pass. That Easthampton readers stayed loyal to the Gazette was entirely due to his highly professional coverage of the town.

Not all the Gazette correspondents of 30 years ago had such high reputations, alas. Sometimes it was only after hours of phone calls and rewriting

by wire-editor Phil Reed that some of their garbled
stories appeared in readable form.   That this was a
frustrating job was apparent by the quiet outbursts
of impatience that sometimes crackled the air over
Phil's desk.

So it must have been a daily pleasure and relief
to get Russ's copy over the teletype, to which
nothing ever needed to be done except add a headline.

The high respect in which Russ was held also
meant that if we came across a story with Easthampton
connections, we didn't pursue it ourselves but handed
it over to Russ. With other towns we had no such
compunctions, but Easthampton was Russ's territory,
and that was that.

Newspaper correspondents like Russ -- the label
"stringer" seems too casual for what he did -- have
relatively little fame outside their own area. Most
of the time that seems fair enough. But when a
correspondent does such an outstanding job of taking
over a town and making it his/her own, it seems as
if they should have more recognition. Surely the
best of them are on a par with editors of country
weeklies, at the very least. But although there are
organizations for editors, I know of none for people
like Russ.

If there is, or someday will be, a hall of fame
for outstanding correspondents, Russ Flanagan's name
should be there, written perhaps in teletype script.

38

Coming out of Forbes Library the other day I noticed a cement block that said "Works Projects Administration" on it, and that started me off on a nostalgia trail that led, strangely enough, back to my own neighborhood.

In case you don't remember, the WPA was one of the Roosevelt programs that gave people jobs during the Depression. I mean the one in the 1930's, not this one.

When I saw those initials I had a sudden vision of hordes of city forefathers planting trees (as it turns out they indeed did plant all those impressive pin oaks at Forbes Library) and fixing streets. How many of my neighbors participated in the project, I wondered, and how did they feel about it?

It was strangely difficult to track down anything specific. The old Gazette historical files -- begun, I was told, by WPA workers -- had no file on the WPA. Forbes Library finally turned up a listing of articles with dates, and I sat down at a microfilm machine, twiddling dials and uttering occasional cries for help.

Most of the Gazette articles on the WPA were pretty cut and dried, and didn't answer my questions about who, where, and when. I already knew why.

But what I did learn was that Northampton originally had the Emergency Relief Administration,

and most of the projects that were being administered
under that were turned over to the WPA on November
22, 1935. It must have meant a happier Thanksgiving
for at least a few families in Northampton.

The first local project to be turned over was a
sewing project employing 62 women. I'd love to know
what they made, where their end-product went, whether
they chatted while they worked, and what they talked
about, whether their husbands were unemployed and
driving them crazy hanging around the house, whether
their children actually did chores -- things like
that.

There were other, larger construction works
around, too, but the WPA was for smaller projects,
under $25,000, with the city contributing five
percent plus materials if they had them.

Although the Gazette articles on the WPA weren't
very forthcoming -- it's strange how much we assume
everyone knows at the time of writing -- it was
intriguing to be suddenly transported back to 1935-37
through the Gazette items, and to get a whiff of what
was going on back then.

There were headlines such as "Miss Earhart
resumes trip," "Sir James Barrie gravely ill," "Boy
camper ill with typhoid after drinking from Connecticut River," "No Nobel peace prize this year,"
"Smith Professors object to Teacher's Oath, after
signing it."

Historical figures still alive on the stage of
life; dangerous diseases that now seem to belong to
other countries, other times; a faint warning of war,
and a foretaste of the McCarthy era: that was life
60-odd years ago.

Then there was Harold Ohrenberger of Dedham,
Mass., who laughed so hard in a movie theater that he
was given a life pass -- and national publicity.

And noted under a photo of a bathing beauty
wearing a suit made of moss: "since moss comes apart

in water, there won't be much swimming..."

I still wanted to know whether there are any residents left who worked in a WPA project, and how well it really worked. After all, we may be doing it again.

On a hunch, I asked my neighbor, John Zyndorski, who's been around here for a longish time, if he knew anyone who had worked in the old WPA.

"Sure, I did myself." Turns out he and his father and two brothers took turns digging ditches on South Street, and cutting cord wood in city wood lots, for the WPA, when he was still in high school.

John also joined the Civilian Conservation Corps, another Rooseveltian project, right out of high school. He and several other local men were sent up to New Hampshire to work, helping build a ski trail and campgrounds near Cathedral of the Pines. They earned $30 a month to start, and $25 of that was sent home.

Talking about it, John sounded a bit nostalgic. "We had basketball teams, boxing teams," he said, remembering those good old days that the history books say were bad old days.

I'm glad someone took the time to put a marker at Forbes Library, all those years ago, to remind us those of difficult, yet hopeful, times. Under projects like CCC and WPA people got a paycheck and the satisfaction that goes with it, they learned skills and responsibility, and a lot of worthwhile things were accomplished. Not a bad epitaph.

39

Spring, when the sump pump goes full-time in my cellar, seems an appropriate time to write about waterways. Specifically canals, those rather astonishing accomplishments of men with shovels and wheelbarrows, that were arteries of commerce before the railroad came along, and which now are either pleasure boat-ways, or rapidly vanishing.

I just got back from a trip to England, where there was no snow, just green grass, hosts of daffodils, and people in shirtsleeves strolling in the parks.

Where my son lives, on the outskirts of London, a lovely canal walk takes you on a short-cut through town, past the former home of Charles and Mary Lamb. Moor hens with their colorful beaks vie with the swans for scraps of bread from the many pedestrians.

In Hemel Hempstead, a friend took me for a walk along the famed and beautiful Grand Union Canal to a local pub that still caters to the summer boating crowd; and another friend with a boat on the Grantham Canal invited me to come aboard.

Closer to home, many Northamptonites are still intrigued by the Northampton-New Haven Canal, which used to run down King Street and across town, commemorated by a plaque at the corner of Main and State Streets, where the canal Mansion House once stood.

Years ago, after our trip down the canal to Windsor Locks had whetted our interest, I took my sons around the countryside looking for vestiges of the old Northampton-New Haven waterway.

We actually found one spot, somewhere around Southampton I think, where there was a dry ditch that didn't look big enough to accommodate a rowboat. However it was in the right place, and, being tired of looking, I proclaimed it the old canal. I hope it was.

I assume Tim's friend Art Donahue (Jr.) from Hastings Heights in Florence, was along on this adventure, and perhaps our exploring was at least partly responsible for a video, "Lost Canals of New England," which was recently produced, photographed and edited by the same Art Donahue.

Art, who now lives near Boston, works for WCVB, where he produces half-hour shows for "Chronicle," the "only locally-produced five-night-a-week news magazine in the country" according to Art. If you've seen "Discover New England," that's mostly repackaged segments from "Chronicle;" next time, look for Art's name among the credits.

Art's sister, who lives in Northampton, had sent him a copy of the column I wrote recently about all the activities in our backyard in Florence, and he had replied with a letter about what he's been up to in recent years. Several of the shows he mentioned working on were ones I'd seen and liked -- New England lighthouses, fall foliage, Boston Harbor islands and many others.

When he mentioned that Forbes Library had copies of "Lost Canals of New England," I went right down to borrow it, glad of a chance to finally see actual photos of the elusive canal.

The tape (which also has segments on the Boston-Lowell canal and the one from Providence to Worcester), was indeed very informative about the Northampton canal.

When built in the early 1800's it was the longest canal in New England -- and became the most disastrous financially. It was 87 miles long, with 60 locks taking the boats up and down 300 feet of altitude. It took 10 years to build -- before mechanized equipment had been invented -- and lasted only 10 years, losing a million dollars for its investors before its right-of-way was sold to the railroads in 1845. The entire canal era was over by 1850.

The wooden aqueduct we canoed across north of Windsor Locks many years ago got me interested in those marvels which have been around since Mesopotamia; the Northampton canal had at least two, the Westfield aqueduct of 300 feet the longest in New England at the time. The other carried the canal via huge stone piers across the river in Farmington. Nothing is left of these aquaducts today, although, as elsewhere, the embankments are still discernible.

Another record-breaker was the floating tow-path across Middle Pond in Southwick, again the largest in New England. This canal's planners weren't afraid to do things big.

The video shows some of the rare spots where the canal is still visible. The most interesting one, which I intend to visit this summer, is lock number 12 in Cheshire, Connecticut, where there is not only a well-preserved canal lock, but even a museum.

A photographic record of the canal was made about 50 years ago, when it had already started to disappear, by photographer Charles Rufus Hart. Today's major canal buff is Carl Walter of Granby, Connecticut, who is making a computer-generated visual record of the canal route.

But none of these records recaptures the excitement people must have felt about traveling down the canal all the way to New Haven. The video mentions honeymooners who would take the canalboat to the big city to buy their furniture and bring it back to their new homes. What an adventure!

Or the excitement of walking along its banks, watching the boats and tow- mules go past, hearing their whistles toot as they rounded the bend (or is this all imagination?). I'm sure there were hundreds of small boys who grew up along its 87-mile length and found it shimmering and beckoning in the back of their minds all the rest of their lives.

There's a satisfaction even today in walking along a canal, even where nothing at all is happening. It's too bad, really, that Northampton has lost forever that romantic, picturesque piece of history.

Yet satisfying that a Northampton native has captured what's left, for us to dream on.

40

Why is that things break down in the middle of the night, when nobody is even looking at them, much less using them?

I woke up around five one recent Friday morning to a strange odor. I lay there, three-quarters asleep, wondering if the smell was coming in from outdoors, in which case I should roust myself out of bed and close the window.

Then I began to realize that the sump pump was pumping water out of my basement on a nearly full-time basis. Was it raining? Didn't look like it, said one eye. Didn't sound like it, said one ear. Was it broken, or something?

I supposed I'd better get up and go look. I got into my bathrobe and slippers and got to my door -- and then I heard the hissing noise in my kitchen.

Oh God, I panicked, the gas is leaking and the house is going to blow up. That's when I woke up in earnest, and half ran, half slithered down the stairs.

Luckily, it wasn't gas, just a fountain of water coming out of the washing machine hose.

I don't remember anyone ever telling me that you're supposed to turn off the washing machine faucets when they aren't in use. Maybe they did, many years ago, but I've never done it -- til now. The water pressure had finally split the hose. I turned off the taps, getting soaked in the process.

With the faucets off, I thought the crisis was over, although my slippers were standing in half an inch of water. The smell was stronger, too. But wait, what was that noise, coming from down cellar? Oh help, was something else broken down there? I yanked open the door and ran down.

You know what it was? Water, pouring through the ceiling, sounding like a heavy rain. I'd never had indoor rain before, but I didn't stop to marvel at it just then.

Reassured that nothing else needed to be turned off, I ran back upstairs, grabbed a broom, and started sweeping water out the back door. If any neighbors were up at that hour, I must have been an interesting sight.

After maybe 15 minutes of that, the rain in the cellar was abating and the kitchen carpet was again visible, though thoroughly soaked. The broom wasn't doing much any more. Time for plan B.

I've had disasters before, so I knew it was time to get out the towels. This was a 14-towel crisis, and I could have used more.

For the next hour I walked barefoot around on the towels, wringing them out the back door in rotation, until my hands were sore and my feet were numb with cold.

The water had spread into my livingroom, so that needed some work, too. There were books and magazines that were wet. Furniture in need of rescue. The stove's electric starter wouldn't work. And it was still two hours before I could phone the plumber.

Eventually I gave up on the towels and threw them all out on the back railing, where it was now raining in the more natural mode.

The plumber, when he finally came, suggested a wet-vac. So as soon as he left, which was after 4 p.m., I grabbed up my coat and dashed out to rent a wet-vac. Only when I got to my car I realized I'd forgotten my keys. Oh, you thought this was a one-disaster day?

The lock experts, when I phoned from a neighbor's, had already closed up for the weekend. I had to break a window in order to get back in.

With more foresight than I'd shown yet that day, I measured the space, so that when I rented the wet-vac I was also able to get a replacement pane next door -- all just before closing.

Back to the house to wet-vac. The outlet on the machine wasn't fully closed and water dribbled out on a dry part of the carpet. But hey, what difference did it make by that time? Then replace the window pane, and collapse into an armchair with the inimitable smell of damp carpet to accompany the evening's boob-tube fare.

In a way, I was lucky. It could have happened the next day, which was my birthday. If it had waited til then, I think I would have cried. I do hope I've cheered you up. It must be nice to know you aren't the only one who has bad days.

41

Sometimes those gremlins just never let up. I had hoped that writing about the flood in my kitchen might appease them, so they'd leave me alone. But the string of disasters just kept on a-comin'.

Since August I've had three broken windows to take care of (only one of which I broke myself, the time I locked myself out of the house); the kitchen flood, of course; two sagging ceilings; two over-flowing toilets; a door that was accidently broken down; a hot-water heater that rusted out; a furnace valve that stopped working; a sewer pipe that had to be replaced, and a hole in the foundation, through which some large animal came blundering in the middle of the night, scaring me out of my wits -- had you noticed they were missing?

And they say disasters come in threes.

It's great being a homeowner. Those of you who claim that title will laugh hollowly, knowing what I mean. Those of you who rent -- be thankful that you don't know what you're missing.

Those last two crises were the most recent, both happening last weekend. There were several men in the front yard excavating under the front steps to get at the old sewer pipes, while another man was in the back, patching the possibly-possum hole. There were big piles of dirt on the sidewalk all weekend, earth-moving equipment parked across the street, sawhorses up to prevent the neighbors from falling into the eight-feet deep hole where the front walk used to be.

Of course that isn't the major inconvenience to having a sewer dug up, but I'll leave that to the imagination.

As for the little visitor I had, I was wakened from a sound sleep at 2 a.m. by the pitter-patter of little feet -- in the wall right next to me. After letting out a few yelps and whimpers, I started banging on the wall and turned on all the lights. Then I started thinking, suppose it's a skunk? I left on the lights, but stopped banging.

I heard him or her galumphing around in the walls again at 4 a.m. and 6 a.m., and didn't get much sleep in between, either.

At dawn's early light I went out looking for the place the visitor could have gotten in, but everything looked pretty tight. It was puzzling. Maybe it was just a fluke, and the visitor wouldn't come back, I wishfully thought.

He came back, all right. What a noise-maker! It's true wishful thinking doesn't help. Another dawn, another inspection tour. This time, I looked down between the cement wall and the back fence, just behind my house, and there was a pile of newly dug dirt.

Aha! I couldn't see the wall directly, but got a mirror out and hung it between the wall and the fence. To my horror, and maybe some secret admiration for its diligence and gall, I saw that something had dug through the crumbling mortar, excavated a large hole, and had obviously kept right on going under the cement sidewalk, into my house.

I started gathering up anything lying around loose, to cover the hole temporarily. Then I had another thought. Sometimes I do have more than one per day. Suppose this animal had been sleeping in my house during the day, and I was just plugging up his escape route? Suppose it was even planning to hibernate there? Uh-oh.

So I left the hole unplugged until 9:30 that night, when I went out in the rain with a flashlight (I'm always wondering what the neighbors must think of my wierd goings-on) and piled up cement blocks, bricks, old boards, and two bags of dead leaves (I know, I know, what good would they do?) until I was satisfied nothing could get in.

Then I sat around tensely, waiting for noises in the wall. They didn't come. Either my plan had worked, or I have Something hibernating in my attic. Perhaps I'll know in six weeks, when it has its periodic walk-about.

Meantime, the mason has come and gone. The excavation crew recemented the basement, relaid the front walk, raked the dirt neatly where my front lawn used to be, and all's quiet -- for the moment.

Let's see, that was four excavators, three plumbers, a glass man, a furnace man, a water-heater installer, a carpenter, a mason -- did I forget anybody? At least you can't say I haven't been contributing to the local economy.

I even managed to be thankful this Thanksgiving weekend. After all, some whole years go by with nary a disaster. The sewer problem came before the ground froze. And if it was a skunk, he never left his calling card.

42

August, when I was a kid, was the month we spent in Maine, at Sebago Lake. My mother had designed and helped build a cottage in East Sebago, and we would drive up from Boston, on old Route One, starting early in the morning.

My mother had begun her carpentry as a teenager, when she had felt sorry for the family cows standing out in the rain, and had built them a cowshed. Just as she finished, she used to tell us, it started to pour. The cows ambled rapidly toward the shed and leaned thankfully against the sides -- but they never actually went in.

Our Sebago house, however, is still lived in. It has a bathroom now, instead of the cobwebby old outhouse, and is winterized for year-round retirement living, but it still bears my mother's unique stamp.

She wanted a spectacular fireplace, and decided to face it with pink quartz. The center stone was a large, diamond-shaped piece of rose quartz, with a secret compartment behind it, lined with a mirror. From upstairs, we could drop a light bulb into the compartment, and the light would glow rosily through the stone.

The last time I visited, the quartz had faded, as it tends to do, but it still had the secret compartment and, I noticed, the blood the mason had left behind from a cut finger, all those years ago.

My brother and I, aged 12 and 8, also helped with the house. We shellacked knot holes, painted the outside, and waxed the interior, including the ceiling, which was an extremely wearisome task.

One job mother gave us was to mix up the cement -- by stomping up and down in it, as they do to mash up grapes in the wine-making process. She must have thought this sounded romantic -- we also washed sheets in the bathtub by this method. But let me tell you, there is little that is romantic about stomping around in cement.

Down a block, across the highway, and a few houses to the left, was a public access to the lake, with a lovely sandy bottom for swimming. I remember spending hours there, learning to swim, building sand castles, canonballing off the raft, getting dunked by neighbor boys, having splash fights, floating on an inner tube in perfect relaxation, enjoying the sparkles of sun on the water.

One August we arrived at the cottage and immediately raced down to the beach. I had put on last year's woolen swimsuit, and as I jumped off the raft, it parted company right at the crotch, and flapped up to my neck like a window blind, both front and back.

I was at a modest age then, and spent what seemed like several chilly hours in the lake before my teasing brother would bring me a towel and I could creep ignominiously home.

There was a home-grown carnival there one summer, with events like foot races, rowing, swimming, and canoe-tilting. I had never canoe-tilted before, or even seen it done, but I won a medal in that, and in rowing, to my great glee.

When a sailing friend came up to visit we rigged a sail on a rowboat and journeyed across the lake to a deserted island for a picnic. It was a great adventure, and to top it off, on the way back we caught a huge salmon.

Many years later, a telemarketer phoned to try to sell us a lot on the same island, and out of nostalgia I invited him to come out and show us his promotional film.

It was disappointing, seeing the unspoiled island of my youth now covered with cottages, and I tried to call a halt, but of course it's pretty hard to get rid of these salesmen once their foot is in your door.

Fortunately, our dishwasher caught fire in mid-film, and he seemed glad to escape out of our driveway before the fire engines roared in.

The relief was on both sides; I think I'll just keep my old memories, thanks.

43

There's a role mothers play, of pretending not be bothered by thunder storms in order to calm the fears of their children. We act serene, divert attention, are generous with hugs. Even if we ourselves were frightened of thunder as children, it works.

Once the children are grown, though, and there's nobody to pretend for, the uneasiness sometimes creeps back. After all, someone we know was killed by lightning; we've seen houses charred and scarred by it; our telephones have rung eerily, the TV has spit sparks, and our faucets have given us shocks. It would be more logical to be nervous than to pretend this isn't an awesome force.

Last Wednesday, though, the storm seemed distant enough not to be alarming, even though the electricity had gone off twice. Standing in my open front door, I was looking for breaks in the clouds and noticing that the rain was letting up, when suddenly there was a sizzle and boom, like a bomb going off nearby.

I leaped back, and then cautiously looked out again. I couldn't see anything, although surely something had been struck. In a very few minutes sirens began coming our way, and two fire trucks roared by.

Fire engines on your own street are a powerful draw, and without even grabbing an umbrella, I dashed out to the sidewalk.

The fire trucks were a few houses away, and firefighters in their black and yellow slickers and helmets were busily unrolling lengths of hose. A knot of people had already gathered, and someone was pointing. Others were coming out to see what was going on. A neighbor muttered something about a camera and dashed inside again. A police cruiser slewed across the road to keep traffic at bay.

The rain had nearly stopped -- for the moment -- and I joined the small stream of people heading up the street. But when I got to where the crowd was watching, I didn't understand what I saw. The roof of a house set back from the street had a plume of smoke rising from it, and beyond that there seemed to be a yellow crane or cherry-picker, half-hidden behind a tree. How had the crane gotten there so fast? Or had it been there already, and had been the attraction for the lightning?

I was totally wrong, of course. The yellowish bars were the bare bones of the pine tree that had been hit, broken, and stripped bare for several feet.

Just then the thunder rolled again, and I leaped onto the nearest porch with hardly a by-your-leave. Funny how something over your head seems safer, even when logic might tell you it was not, if you were listening to logic.

Neighbors who hardly saw each other were now conversing as if they were old friends, drawn together in part curiosity, part sympathy, part the impulse to offer help.

I decided to go around the corner for a better view, although the rain had started to increase its volume. The fire in the roof had already been put out; the forlorn pine was shapeless behind the debris from its upper branches; shingles that had been blown off the roof lay scattered around the yard, 20 or 30 feet away. Among several knots of people, the inhabitants of the house stood huddled in a daze, shocked by the sudden disaster but no doubt very aware of their close shave in escaping something worse.

The neighbor with the camera appeared and took photos. More umbrellas went up, and I was beginning to feel wet. I walked on back home, jumping over fire hoses, waving to those kind neighbors whose porch had sheltered me.

A sense of community, it seems, lurks just below the surface of a neighborhood. There's some comfort in glimpsing it, even though it may take a lightning-stroke to make us realize it's there.

44

I've just finished reading the enjoyable new book by local auctioneer Bill Hubbard, "Auction: or 'Madame, you cannot possibly go wrong on this bed.'" The latter is a quote from another local auctioneer, Ray Murphy.

Ah, the memories it brought back! Auctions can be great fun, as we learned when we bought a house in Scotland and, not knowing whether we would ever live in it, wanted to furnish it inexpensively.

We drove off to Elgin, as green as any auctioneer could possibly wish. While Alec went to make friends with the managers, I looked helplessly at the mountain of furniture, piled higgledy-piggledy up to the ceiling.

Almost the first item called was a set of five chairs. The bidding started at a couple of cents a chair, and we got them for ten cents each.

We thought we were well on our way, but the next lot was another five chairs, in much better condition. We got those for ten cents apiece, too.

The chairs kept getting better, and we kept on buying them. Our top price was twenty cents each, and those were actually presentable.

We ended up with a garage full of chairs. Luckily, a friend of ours opened a tearoom several months later, and we donated all the extras.

We probably furnished our five-room house (plus the garage) for about $500, including oriental rugs, brand new beds, each with one slat broken, several huge oak tables, an ugly livingroom set, and a railway station clock.

By the time we had filled the house, we had the auction bug. Getting a good bargain was like winning the lottery, and for Americans in Britain in 1973, everything seemed like a good bargain.

Once we bought a rather unusual item. Our youngest son had come with us, and when they announced they had six rabbits for sale, James was down on his knees, pleading with us to get one. I think it cost 30 cents. James named it Speedy Gonzales, and it thrived on dandelion leaves.

Then auction prices started heading upward. London antique dealers got wind of our area, and there was no point trying to outbid them.

One of the last times I bought something, the auctioneer quite obviously pretended to get a bid across the room in order to then stick me with a higher price. I ended up with some brocaded draperies so heavy they pulled the fixtures off the wall, and a sovereign case with a broken clasp. I was annoyed, but didn't stay that way; I waited a few weeks, put the items back into the auction, and came out of it $15 ahead!

The last auction I went to was when Cullen House, the crenelated home of the Earl and Countess of Seafield, was being sold, and its contents auctioned off. Christies, the famous London auction house, was selling off the contents of the "castle," and expecting over two million dollars. In the event, they only got about $600,000, but that gives you some idea of the contents and the interest they aroused.

There were a number of different auctions going on throughout the edifice, but I chose to go to the huge, paneled library, where they were selling off the books. Most were either very dull or obviously valuable. However, I had located a book which contained one spectacular illuminated letter, but was not listed that way; it seemed possible the volume would be overlooked. A London antique dealer was my only rival, but they never give up. She got the book as soon as I stopped bidding, and I ruefully realized that all I had done was raise the price and put a little more money in the Earl's pocket.

That was it. Auctions had gone beyond my price range, and I never went again. But darn, they were fun while I lasted. After reading Hubbard's book, I'm tempted to dip my toes in again. Someday soon I may be going, going, gone.

45

You've seen those ads: "I was near bankruptcy, my car was repossessed, I lost my house -- but now I bank a million dollars a month..." I think the same man writes them all.

Well, we all make mistakes. I answered the one about "billions of dollars of your money lies in government vaults. Help people get their money back and earn a finder's fee." Sounds noble, doesn't it?

Following instructions, I wrote to the state division of so-called "abandoned property," and bought a set of microfiches containing 23,296 names of Massachusetts people who currently have lost anywhere from $1.18 to thousands of dollars. Why did they lose it? The state took it, that's why. Be sure you go in and put your passbook through the bank system every year or two, or you may lose your savings, too.

I must have looked up about 300 of those names in the telephone books at Forbes Library. Surprisingly, I found about 200, and of those maybe 50 were still at the same address.

This in spite of the law that says banks must make a reasonable effort to locate customers whose accounts they're about to lift.

There were also quite a few that were listed as "address unknown" but were perfectly obvious, names like Harvard College Libraries, Town of Lincoln, City of Lynn, Milton Public Library, Our Redeemer Lutheran Church; City of Peabody, Town of Plymouth; Postmaster, New Orleans, Louisiana; Worcester City Hospital.

Come on!

I photocopied agreements and forms and sent out a mailing. As soon as I got a reply, I sent it on to the state office.

Oh, they said, didn't we give you the right forms? I gritted my teeth. So I started in all over again, with the right forms.

Even though I said to send no fee unless you get your money back, one lady sent me a check for $250, saying that she had been trying for years to pry the money out of the bank, and maybe I'd have better luck. I never cashed the check, because I didn't have any luck, either.

One of the banks insisted they had to know the date the account was taken, although the state office said you didn't need it -- and doesn't give you the date anyway.

I think some of the people I wrote to went and got their money on their own. Good luck to them.

As time went on, I began to realize that I hadn't yet banked a million dollars a month. I hadn't banked one cent.

There was plenty going out, though, in postage and photocopies and phone calls.

I decided to call it quits, but I wrote one last time to the ten or so most hopeful ones, and eventually I did get 'a small finder's fee from two organizations, which let me about break even.

When the Better Business Bureau in Springfield phoned to say someone had inquired whether my heir-finding business was legitimate, I laughed hollowly. Why would anyone crooked be in this business? There's no money in it.

Personally, I think it's criminal that the government has been allowed to take over all these accounts. It seems scandalous that people could lose $5,000 overnight.

But I'm especially sorry for all those little $30 to $40 sums which may mean a lot to students, the elderly, the unemployed. I picture little old ladies with bad memories; college funds started for babies by proud grandparents; a newscarrier's savings; a birthday present for a high school student; or an inheritance the heir never got.

The chances are the real owners will never see that $40. The heir-finders can't be bothered with such small amounts; the state office might not send them the right forms; the banks may give them a hard time.

I've read that the reason this practice started in the first place is that Howard Hughes had put millions of dollars into different accounts, under different names, all across the country.

Okay, but the government must have collected all that by now, so why do they keep on doing it? It's not fair. One might even call it larceny.

Did you ever start a nest-egg account, and find it had disappeared just because it hadn't seen any "action" for a couple of years? Tell you what: I'll donate those microfiches to Forbes Library, and you can go and see if your name is on them. If it is, write to the State Treasury, Unclaimed Property Division, 50 Franklin St., Boston, MA 02110, for a claim form.

Maybe if enough of us get angry at this practice, we can even get it stopped.

46

Nature plays its little jokes with us. How often has it rained on our parade, or refused to snow for a winter carnival? Maybe Native Americans have the right idea, with their rain dances and such. Would it help if Northampton held a snow dance next year, before the winter carnival?

I grew up thinking I had seen snow deep enough to be over my head. Then I realized I had been a lot shorter back then (this is what's known as a short memory).

But looking around this winter, I realize that I was right the first time -- snow definitely used to be deeper. You couldn't see the grass through it. You had to tunnel your way out to the garage. Snowmen sprang up in every yard, and snow forts armed with neat piles of snowballs faced off across every street.

My brother once built a snow house big enough to stand up in. It was glazed with ice to keep other kids from smashing it down, and it even had a glass window for lighting. I was only allowed in it once.

Years later, I used to take my own kids to the Big Y parking lot, where gigantic towers of snow were great places for sliding or for digging out a snow house. Since they weren't in our own yard, they never lasted long, but the fun was in the building.

As for skiing -- I went to a skiing high school in Maine, with ski meets nearly every weekend through the winter. I was in the beginners class for four years, which was a bit off-putting. Of course, it didn't help that the first time I went out to a ski meet, I ended up in the infirmary with bronchial pneumonia. That was off-putting, too.

My senior year, I finally went with some friends up to one of the ski hills near the campus. Just looking down Devil's Hill made me feel sick. Even my friends, who had put beginners class far behind them, didn't attempt it. The amazing thing was that, skiing back down the trail through the woods, I managed the whole thing, leaving only one "bathtub" behind as a memento. It was exhilirating, and I began to think I might begin to like this sport after all.

However, I never went skiing again. Needing money my first year in college, I took my skis in to the Commons at Boston U. one morning and shouted "Skis, five dollars!" They were gone in 10 seconds.

As for sledding, we used to be able to slide down the roads in winter, where I grew up in Maine. By the time my kids came along, the roads were out. We used to go to Hospital Hill, or the hill at Look Park (which I was sissy enough to prefer -- Hospital Hill is steep enough to leave my stomach behind). We'd spend hours tramping up through the snow, and only seconds whizzing down. Sometimes you have to wonder if that's really worth it.

Snow is a wonderful medium for sculpture. There have been some marvels created here in Northampton, as well as elsewhere. But nothing seems more popular than the ubiquitous snowman with the carrot nose, old hat, and scarf. They used to have coal eyes, but I guess that's a thing of the past.

We even used to eat snow, with maple syrup on it, for a special treat. It used to be that clean.

Every New Englander has some fond memories of snow, regardless of how that may change when he or she starts driving in it. My own best memories are of being out in the snow at night, when the air seems crisp and clean, the stars sparkle, and the moonlight reflecting on the snow creates a sense of magic. Add a red and green curtain of northern lights, and the magic is complete.

Nature may play jokes on us, but it gives bountifully in exchange.

47

Our music composition class had its spring concert at Sage Hall last weekend, and we felt pretty pleased with ourselves. Pleased with the volunteer performers, too, who made actual music out of our henscratched sheets of paper.

It was easy to tell whose piece was being performed, by picking out the face showing the most concentration, suppressed excitement, and panic.

What a lovely experience, hearing people playing your music. Am I wrong, or does music/crafts/art play a definite role in therapy programs? Sort of makes you suspect that music/crafts/art is something that is meant to be part of living, if it makes a fractured person whole. I suspect that the obverse is also true, that a lack of creative self-expression makes a person incomplete.

Part of growing up, for all but a few, is learning that you are never going to make it into the big time. Childish dreams of being a famous writer, composer, artist, or rock star, have to be abandoned for most of us. But in the abandoning process, too many of us stop trying altogether. In our competitive society, there are no kudos for the second-rate, and nobody likes the feeling of failure.

Sometimes I think the main job of adult living is unlearning all the wrong things you learned in childhood. It took me years to get to the point where I could enjoy doing things at which I was mediocre. It helped that there were inexpensive courses in a great variety of crafts. I took courses in pottery, ceramics, woodworking, jewelry-making, rock polishing, silk-screening, wood-block printing, stained glass. Just because I didn't turn professional with any of them doesn't mean I didn't thoroughly enjoy myself.

And music. I've written little ditties for as long as I can remember. I'm never going to be a famous musician, that's a sure bet. But so what?

"Amateur" means one who loves. To work at creating something of beauty just for the love of it seems too worthwhile to deserve the low status that it has. While television has done us a great service in bringing us the best artists in the world, it has also done us a disservice, in squashing the small ambitions of the amateur.

We all have gifts, whether they be large or small, and when we exercise those gifts, it feels good. Picture a world in which everyone has the time and opportunity to use those gifts, for their own well-being and for the benefit of all of us. Whole, integrated people, singing as they work. It's a far cry from quiet desperation.

There are too many people, even in this country, for whom just scraping by with a bare living takes all the time and energy they have. All of us are that much poorer because of the hidden gifts that such people fail to contribute to the community.

A society that encourages the best from all of us is the richest society. It's just plain short-sighted for governments to allow poverty, homelessness, hopelessness. The lost opportunities of a present-day Mozart or Van Gogh impoverish us all. (Not to mention that homeless people don't often buy refrigerators.)

I think it was Malcolm Muggeridge, the eminent British writer, who once admitted that in his student years he had been drawn to the Marxist theory that

money is what motivates everone and everything.
"Then one day," added Muggeridge, "I realized I was
spending all my money on something that gave me no
financial return whatsoever -- women." That was the
end of his Marxist period.

Money simply doesn't motivate people to write
music or create other works of art. It's nice if
money rolls in, but it isn't the prime mover. The
students in the music course, for instance, got no
money from their work. Writing music brought them
little more than inner satisfaction, a mark on a
report card that will be meaningless a few years from
now, and perhaps a few praises from their peers.

But I'm here to tell you that there are other
things writing music can bring you.

I had some songs published in a songbook in
Britain. One day my son Tim heard a young woman
playing a tune on her recorder, and he went up to
her. "My mother wrote that," said he. A year later
they were married, and now have two children.

See? Writing music can also bring you grand-
daughters.

48

It's not often I get a check for $1,000 in the mail. Naturally there was a catch to it. I could use it toward buying a car down in Springfield the following Wednesday. Worth $2,000 toward a used car. Even as I scoffed, I admired the ingenuity of it all.

I looked at my trusty old Rabbit. True, the neighbors made a show of blocking their ears when we chugged by. True, its visits to the car doctor seemed to be increasing. True, trying to find diesel fuel when traveling was something of a challenge.

But on the other hand, it was dependable; it was cute; it had plenty of miles yet to go; it was fuel efficient -- you can't beat 45 miles to the gallon.

I looked at the dazzling check again. Well, I thought, I suppose it's possible they've got something I'd like down there -- newer, with fewer miles. With $2,000 off the top and something as trade-in for my Rabbit, I might get a good deal. It wouldn't hurt to look, would it?

I can hear you yelling, "Sucker bait!" How could a cynic like me actually be falling for this?

On the day of the sale, I drove down. I thought there might be hordes of buyers, but the economy must have kept them at home. There was only one man ahead of me at the welcome table, where a hostess was writing down names and addresses and giving out presents.

Then I was introduced to my own personal salesman, Bob.

"What kind of car are you looking for?" said he.

"Cheap," said I.

We looked over the list of used cars, and there were only five under $6,000. I decided right then I wasn't buying a car that day. But I had time, I'd look.

One car was newer, but had more miles on it than my Rabbit.

One we couldn't find.

One was really a higher price.

One, we were told as we walked up to it, had just been sold.

That left one, and it was an '87 Subaru with only 53,000 miles on it. The trouble was, it was a wagon. What would I want with a wagon? I like compacts.

Mumbling negatively, I agreed to test drive it, but did so only half-heartedly, around the block.

"I don't think I want it," I said.

Since there were no other cars, we went inside to talk things over. Despite its sticker price of $5995, I felt in my bones this was a $3500 car, maybe a little more. (I was right, I learned later. The book price was $3625.) I had expected the $2,000 come-on to be added to the price, and yet at the same time it was hard for me to believe it could have been done so blatantly. That's a 60 per cent uplift.

"How much would you give me for the Rabbit?"

Bob went away to consult and came back with a $700 figure. With the $2,000 off, the price was now down to $3295. Too much.

I shook my head. "We're never going to get close to my figure."

"Which is?"

"Under $2,000."

Bob consulted again and came back with $2600. I shook my head again. "When I said under $2,000, I didn't mean I'd meet your price halfway, I meant under $2,000. I shouldn't take up any more of your time."

"No, no," said Bob gently, "let me ask again."

This time the price was $2300.

"It's not as if I really even want the car," I grumbled. "A wagon would mean cleaning out another two feet of space in my garage." I shuddered at the thought of all that work. "Well, let me think about it."

And I thought about it. It was upgrading my car by five years; it looked good, and was rust-proofed, which the Rabbit wasn't; it had a 60-day warranty, so I had some protection; even if I didn't want a wagon, perhaps I could think of ways to utilize it.

I went to look for Bob. "I'd take it for $2200," I said. His boss shrugged. "Write it up."

So that's how come you can't hear me coming any more. I have yet to learn whether this car tastes like lemonade in the rain, but so far so good.

I guess the time to buy a car is when you don't really care if you buy it or not. But am I a sucker anyway, for upgrading when I wasn't really ready? For buying a wagon I don't really want? You decide. But don't let me know.

49

Every now and then we hear tales of technology gone mad, like the stories of banks spewing out million-dollar windfalls to unsuspecting depositors. Aside from hoping it will happen to us, we mostly feel resignation. When we make mistakes, we get the blame, but when machines do -- we still get the blame.

On a certain level, it usually is true that it isn't computers that make mistakes, it's people, feeding wrong information into them.

But here's the whole crux of the matter: people do make mistakes. Why do we keep failing to take this into account when we set up our world? Where there's no room to allow for human error, things could go wrong in a big way.

The other day I heard the perfect example of great technology mixing with human ignorance. It produced something rather weird and wonderful, but let's not forget it could be a lot more serious than this.

What happened was that one night the phone rang at two a.m. at a friend's house, and a sleepy husband picked up the phone.

It was the weather service. You know, the recorded message one, that you have to phone for information. No way, you say, can the recorded message call you, right? That's what he thought, sitting there with a stunned expression.

Well, there is a perfectly logical explanation. The couple had a house-guest, whose wife was arriving somewhere at 2 a.m. and was then going to call her husband.

The guest, not wanting his hosts to be disturbed at 2 a.m. by the phone ringing, had a brilliant idea. He made sure his friends had "call waiting" service, which gives you a beep when another call is coming in.

Then at about 1:45 a.m. he dialed the weather service, and while getting the latest on barometric pressure, waited to hear the beep. It came, it was his wife, they had a short conversation, and then he hung up and went upstairs to bed.

He shouldn't have hung up. The weather service was still on the system, and the only way it could respond was to ring back. See? Perfectly logical.

We humans really are an inventive lot. We have wonderful ideas. In fact, "call waiting" may have resulted from an idea of my own.

Years ago I wrote to the phone company suggesting that the subscriber should have more control over whom he or she wants to talk to. Why should we be at the mercy of any telemarketer, wrong number, or heavy breather who dials us?

Before you even pick up the receiver, a little screen should give the number that's calling, so you can decide whether or not you want to answer.

The screen could also tell you if and when someone is trying to reach you while you're talking with someone else (call waiting, but better).

It could record who called you while you were out.

And it would essentially put an end to crank calls, because you would know immediately which phone the crank was calling from.

The phone company wrote back saying that such a thing was utterly impossible. Now they're starting to do most of it, one way or another.   But they're taking all the credit.

People being inventive, we will often use something in a way not foreseen by the inventor. The better technology gets, the more margin for error there seems to be for human forgetfulness, fumbling, and even misplaced ingenuity.

Perhaps if we were really ingenious we would build more fumble-factors into our wonderful gadgets. Or else learn to really enjoy it when the weather service phones in the dead of night.

50

I may have traveled quite a bit, but this summer I found adventure in some quite inexpensive jaunts right here in Massachusetts.

In Boston for a week to stay with a friend, we decided to go visit Nantucket. It meant getting up at 5:30 a.m., but it was worth it.

We set off for Hyannis at 6:30, caught the 9:15 boat ($9.50 each way, car parking $7), and enjoyed a very smooth trip across sparkling waters to Nantucket, eating a picnic lunch on board as we got near.

Since my friend had never been there, we took an entertaining bus tour around the island ($9 each), and then spent three leisurely hours walking around town, admiring the cobblestone streets lined with gracious buildings, shady trees, and convenient benches.

I had been there 20 years ago with my husband and youngest son, and had been hankering to go back ever since. It has such an air of elegance yet simplicity, of charm yet sobriety, with traditions of Quaker integrity and whaling adventure, island isolation coupled with bustling cosmopolitan polish.

We missed some excitement by inches. Three fishermen who had lost their boat and had been adrift in a life raft for five days were picked up and brought in to the harbor just ahead of us.

We had also just missed an interesting 150th anniversary. I had never associated the famed abolitionist, Frederick Douglass, with Nantucket, but it seems that he made his first speech to a white audience there, at the nation's first anti-slavery convention. Douglass spoke so eloquently of his own experiences as a slave, from which he had escaped shortly before, that it moved many Nantucketers to the abolitionist movement.

Nantucket was an island of independent-minded people, including Ben Franklin's mother and the early woman's rights advocate Lucretia Mott. It has some of that independent spirit still. A wonderful place to visit.

Two days later, we drove up to Rockport for the day, on Cape Ann. Rockport is another place I love to go, specifically for the picturesque ambiance of Bear's Neck, a narrow isthmus about wide enough for a footpath and lined on both sides with tiny shops of great variety. In a way, it's like an outdoor museum, with art galleries and craft shops exhibiting wonderful creations.

But there are also Chinese shops with exotic but inexpensive clothes; toy shops with rainbow whales and model fishing boats; gemstones and scrimshaw, photographers where you dress up in oldfashioned costumes and get a sepia print; restaurants and strudel stands and ice cream shops, and all of it pleasing to the eye. Down at the end there's a place with benches, for landbound people like us who like to sit and stare at the sea.

We had lunch at the Blacksmith Shop (around $10 each), right in an open window overlooking the harbor, with the sound of lapping water, seagull cries, and bell buoys wafting in on the ocean breeze.

The third adventure was closer to home. A lot closer. In fact, it was the "Taste of Northampton" right down there in the parking lot behind Main Street. Much as residents of Nantucket and Rockport bemoan the thousands of tourists that invade them every summer, there's something about a happy crowd that makes a place lively and exciting, and gets you out of the summer doldrums.

For just a few 50 cent tokens, I sampled some peanut chicken from East Side Grill, some Dutch orange chocolate ice cream from Herrell's, a variety of tempting aromas, and what must surely be a new mood for the parking lot.

We even get some of that flavor at the Farmer's Market, downtown every Saturday morning through the summer. Travel may be fun, and broadening to the mind and hips, but staying right here can be an adventure, too.

51

This is not only the season of graduations, it's the season of reunions. Classmates who have avoided each other for 40 years turn up and find it's fun, or maybé not, to meet again, compare notes, count off children, euphemize jobs.

Williston-Northampton School in Easthampton had a reunion weekend last week, and as a former faculty member of Northampton School for Girls (which merged with Williston about 20 years ago) I was invited.

Though my own reunions are a lot of fun, I have to admit that Williston-Northampton's have a lot more meat to them. They actually assume their graduates still have an interest in the world.

Consequently, they had a group of seminars Friday afternoon and Saturday. Some of the topics you could choose from were "The Modernization of China and Taiwan," led by two faculty members who had had semesters in Taiwan in recent years, one of whom had led a student trip to Hong Kong and China this year; "On Writing and the Teaching of it," led by faculty members Ellis Baker and Barry Moser; "The Art of the Northwest Coast Indians;" "Biomedical Ethics of the 90's;" "The Soviet Union in Transition;" "Major League Baseball," led by Steve August, class of '72, traveling secretary for the Boston Red Sox, and "Election 1992 Conventional Wisdom: Is it Suspect?" with faculty member Peter Gunn and alum Jeff Alderman, director of polling at ABC News.

Whoever planned all this was right -- the seminars were lively and interesting. Did you know that all three front-running presidential candidates are left-handed?

The weekend events also included exercise -- a golf outing, yoga before breakfast, student-faculty baseball and volleyball games, swimming, walks, a seminar on exercise, and let's not forget dancing til midnight.

Lunch on Saturday, originally intended for the lawn, was held in the new gym, where the snappy music of a strolling jazz band (except I didn't see them stroll) kept the energy level high. There was even a swan carved in ice. Periodic announcements drew alumni to the balcony for class photos.

At a tea for the former Northampton School for Girls alumnae I spread out a batch of photos I had taken as publicity director there, many of them of students from this area, which brought on reminiscences of absent classmates.

Some were photos of a trip to Broadway, but where was the photo I took of Mohammed Ali, who was staying at our hotel? It must have been put in a special place, and you know what happens then.

Former faculty members Helene Cantarella and Virginia Grahame arrived, and were soon centers of small groups remembering the good old days at the Northampton campus on Pomeroy Terrace: the graduations on the lawn, with girls in white dresses each carrying a long-stemmed rose; the angelus bell, the field hockey games in the meadows, the annual medieval banquet, the plays and glee club concerts and student pranks in class.

No one mentioned, but I remembered, the time a faculty member's Christmas present from her class was a sock with a lump of coal in it -- the French gift (or more often just a threat) for a naughty child. It brought down the house.

If I sound nostalgic, I was a little. But I was jolted back to the present when I got home after the tea. Sailing majestically past my house was a huge hot air balloon.

They didn't have those at Northampton School for Girls. In fact, they had darn little hot air there at all.

52

The new fence is up on the bike-path bridge; I even picked up a piece of it -- a clipped-off end that was lying on the walk -- for my collection, if three pieces make a collection. The other two are a piece of the Greenham Common fence in England, which peaceniks used to cut at any opportunity, and a piece of the Berlin Wall. Not all fences make good neighbors.

In my first few visits to the bike-path bridge there were several young men and even two quite young girls leaping off the span into the river. It was rather fun to watch, but scary. Given human propensity for pushing any limits, it's doubtful the new fence will prevent these high jumps, but it may keep toddlers from falling off.

My first reconnaissance was on a Sunday evening in August, while the sun was still strong. There were dozens and dozens of walkers, cyclists, baby strollers, skateboarders, and even one wheelchair on the boardwalk, and most people had a surprised grin on their faces. After all, this is not only something new, it is also an extremely pleasant place to be.

Besides the divers to watch, there were the campers on Ellwell's Island, the variety of boats zooming up and down the water, the maneuverings at the Sportsman's Marina, frolicking kids, and even a heron sitting nonchalantly under the Coolidge Bridge amid all this activity.

As you start across from the Northampton side, the branches meet overhead, giving a shady tree-house effect as you walk several feet above the ground. On the shore beneath the bridge a dock seems to be a popular place for fishing. Ellwell Island has a feeling of remoteness, inhabited only by birds and insects, despite its summer quota of campers on the sandy beach.

Then comes the busy river, at a level that gives you a better chance to see and appreciate what's going on. And at the Hadley end, the bike path disappears around a long, wooded curve, between Route 9 businesses and corn fields, to lure you toward Amherst.

Northampton, I've noticed, is rather limited as far as bodies of water go. Even Leeds' swimming hole is small. Aside from the Forbes Library driveway (now fixed), the swamp behind St. Michaels (now fixed), and my basement (now fixed), what lakes has Northampton got? Even Look Park pool is on its way out. The bike path is going to be very popular with those of us who have to go look at water every now and then.

One thing the railroad bridge has provided for several generations of kids, was a way to get out to the island without a boat. A steel hawser down one of the stone supports was the semi-secret route.

The new fence will make that route more difficult, and more dangerous, and one wonders whether the planners gave any consideration to making a better access down to the island, instead of virtually closing it off.

I went down to the bridge yesterday to see how it looked on a weekday afternoon after school had started. The walkers and bicyclists were 50-50, eight each, although six more walkers were about to enter it as I left.

The island has been abandoned by all the summer

swimmers, and the shore birds have reclaimed it. The water highway was quiet, the boats at the marina bobbing up and down quiescently. The swimmers were absent, the wind still, the ducks slow-moving. All very peaceful.

It reminded me that the population of the world has more than doubled since I was born, and that the way things are going, one can unfortunately picture a world in which there are no more peaceful, wild, natural sites where one can go strolling on a summer evening. It makes me very thankful that someone got this great idea, and it was followed through.

The bike commuters would like it all for themselves, but they don't need to take over the bridge for every hour of the day. What if there were posted "commuter hours," say from 8 to 9 a.m. and 5 to 6 p.m. on weekdays, when cyclists would have the right of way and pedestrians would be asked to keep clear or to enter the bridge at their own risk; the rest of the time pedestrians could have the right of way and cyclists would have to slow down.

Most people who want to walk on the bridge could surely accommodate themselves to that schedule, allowing all parties to have what they want.

Meanwhile, my thanks to everyone involved in creating this new area. May we all be smart enough to keep it safe, and may it long provide enjoyment.

53

I don't suppose many people here in the valley realize that I was once a television newscaster.

To understand how such a thing could happen, you have to know that way back then, the Gazette, WHMP and Channel 40 had a certain closeness and cooperation among the three. We at the Gazette made carbon copies of our stories for WHMP, and they kept us posted on stories they were doing.

Come to think of it, a lot of our news-gathering was circular that way. Of course, we covered city government meetings and other city events in person, but sometimes it seemed as if we got most of our news from the Springfield morning paper. On those exciting days when I substituted for the city editor, my first job on arrival at the office at 5 a.m. was to cut up the Springfield paper and parcel out the stories to the rest of the staff, for them to update and rewrite.

I felt less concerned about this practice when I went to the Union's Northampton office one day and found them cutting up the Gazette for the same purpose.

But to get back to television. Someone at Channel 40 got the bright idea of giving Northampton news more of a local flavor by bringing a remote crew up to Northampton once or twice a week and using Gazette reporters to do the broadcast.

There was some excitement that first day when the van came up and the TV crew bundled Don Ebbeling out to the parking lot for a news broadcast. We could hardly wait for the TV news that night, and there was a lot of good-natured kidding in the office next morning.

But the following week it wasn't Don, it was someone else, probably Bernie Decker. And the week after that, they asked me if I'd like to do it.

"What's going on?" I asked Don. He leaned over and whispered conspiratorially, "They don't pay."

He went on to suggest that if we all refused to do it gratis, they might start to discuss remuneration. He seemed to think I should do this before I did a broadcast, but the lure of the bright lights was too strong. Besides, they had both done it for nothing once; surely I could, too.

However, a look in the mirror made me shudder. You may have heard women say this before -- "my hair is a mess" -- but I wasn't kidding.

I called one of those places optimistically called a beauty parlor, arranged for a quick image enhancement, and dashed out.

That was the 60s, and the beautician arranged my hair bouffant style, but with a big hole in the front, sort of like a bird's nest standing on edge. It looked peculiar to me, but I was in a hurry, and nervous, and besides I wasn't sure there was a better alternative, so I 'let it go. It was sprayed with that no-nonsense spray they used back then, under which no hair dared to move, nor in fact could.

I ran back to the Gazette, expecting to be filmed in the parking lot, but instead they took me up to the Hampshire County San in Leeds, which is on top of a windy hill. Did I mention it was winter? The bird's nest swayed disconcertingly in the breeze, and some chickadees seemed to be taking an undue interest in it.

The taping began, and it was soon discovered that I had a big drawback as a TV newsperson. Whenever I fumbled, which was fairly often, I couldn't seem to help making a face about it. Whereas what they wanted was for me to take it in my stride and just keep going. We took several takes, but finally the ordeal was over. I was beginning to see why the other reporters didn't want to do this without getting paid.

When I got back, the three of us veterans banded together and asked about possible financial arrangements, with the result that Channel 40 decided to stop coming up.

That night I seated my kids in front of the TV, got my camera ready, and got a picture of me and the bird's nest on the boob tube, a rare photo since that was not only my debut but my final appearance. Well, I did tell you I was "once" a TV newscaster.

I put down my camera, full of pride, though with a few niggling doubts about my hairdo.

"Well, kids, what did you think of Mom on television?"

"Can we eat now?"

So much for fame.

54

I see Northampton's radio station WHMP is planning to go all talk. Another of many changes that have taken place over the years since WHMP first went on the air, Dec. 3, 1950.

I've always taken a particular interest in the station, since it was my husband Alec who, as its first manager, got it on the air. My kids grew up on tales of those early days.

I got more of a peek into the world of radio when Alec became president of the Massachusetts Broadcasters Assn. and we went to Washington for a meeting of the national association. There we traded stories with Fred Friendly, John Chancellor, and many other famous newsmen, got passes to the press box at the Senate, and in general had a better time than you would have supposed by the flight down, which had us stacked up over National Airport for several hours.

When WHMP first went on the air, they had music all right -- but only one record. The staff, and probably the listeners, got heartily sick of "Begin the Beguine" before they raised enough money from advertising to buy a few more records.

Joe Fennessey, who started off with Alec at the beginning, had the morning shift. Several months after the opening, Alec was horrified to realize that Joe, who had an artifical leg, was climbing the four flights of stairs to the top floor of 78 Main Street every morning, because he arrived earlier than the elevator operator. Joe never mentioned it, but Alec got him a key to the elevator just the same.

I just drove downtown to see whether you could still see the shadow of where the WHMP neon sign used to be, on the exterior of 78 Main. You can't. The building looks freshly cleaned. But when Alec first turned on the sign, he decided that rather than turn it off every night, he'd leave it on and see how long it lasted. Well, it lasted at 25 or 30 years, until the station moved to its present quarters on Hamden Avenue.

Grace Gordon, who died a few weeks ago, was another long-time staffer at the station, and I remember her telling me at our wedding that Alec was a sweetheart to work for. Later, when she told me of some occasion when this was not necessarily so, I reminded her of what she said. "You don't want to believe everything people tell you at your wedding," she retorted.

Perhaps not many people realize what a rarity Ron Hall is. Radio newsmen are by tradition, and apparently inclination, people who jump around from place to place, station to station. Very few stay put in one place. But Ron Hall became a newsman at WHMP 35 years ago, his voice becoming a familiar sound to a couple of generations in the Pioneer Valley. That must be one for the records.

Andy Wiernasz is another long-time early staffer at WHMP, among many who came and went, and sometimes came and went again, that I particularly remember. Andy, in his rather quiet way, could sell refrigerators to Eskimos. Alec firmly believed that Andy knew everyone in the Pioneer Valley, and perhaps it was true. Andy also dominated the polka scene on WHMP for many years.

One of Alec's WHMP stories has overtones of an O. Henry story about human erring and remorse. The station used to hold a turkey raffle every Christmas. One year during a near-blizzard Alec was alone at the station on Christmas eve, with only one task left before he could go home: to draw the winning ticket and deliver the turkey.

The winner was a man way up in the hills, and Alec looked out the window at the swirling snow and icy roads, and then looked again at the box full of tickets. Rather furtively and ashamedly, he pulled another ticket, and this time it was someone who lived closer to home. Alec announced him as the winner and went out to deliver the turkey and then hurry home for his own Christmas celebrations.

Later, Alec learned that the man up in the hills was really down on his luck, had a large family, and had recently lost his job. Alec felt terrible about what he had done. For years afterward, every Christmas, he would bemoan the fact that he hadn't played fair. At least the incident guaranteed that it would never happen again.

When the new FM tower went up on Horse Mountain, we could see the new red light atop the tower from our kitchen window in Florence. So it was actually our own eyes and not some technical mechanism, that warned us the time the tower froze up and the lights went out, and the time one of the engineers lit a fire up there to keep warm, and failed to realize he hadn't gotten it all out when he left.

I remember Alec telling me he was thrilled one of those early days, to look down at the traffic on Main Street from his corner office and actually see someone tapping out, on the roof of his car, the rhythm of the music they were playing. It meant someone was actually listening -- something he hadn't really been totally convinced of until then.

Now that the station is scrapping most of its music, that's a sight you won't see again. But I wonder what will become of what must be a rather large music record library by now?

And somewhere in a dusty box marked "don't play," do they still have "Begin the Beguine?"

55

Remember back at the end of 1989 when everyone was writing about the story of the year, the story of the decade, or the story you're most sick of hearing? I can hardly wait for 1999, when people start trying to figure out the story of the century.

For me, the story of the 1980s decade is one that hasn't yet been told. It's the story about how a handful, and then hundreds, and then thousands of ordinary Americans refused to believe that we had to have enemies, and live with the threat of nuclear war.

Those ordinary Americans adopted sister cities in the USSR, as Northampton did, and wrote letters, sent photos, got their kids to send drawings. They went over to see the Russians for themselves, first a trickle and then a flood. They invited Russians back over here. They went to Nicaragua, too, and probably prevented the US from invading that country, just by being there.

Hundreds of kids have also participated in this people-to-people exchange. Groups like Children's Art Exchange in Vermont, and "Drawing Together" in Deerfield, sent children's drawings. Scores of kids went to the USSR to act in the musical "Peace Child," with mixed Soviet and American casts. The National Storyteller's Association sent a group of kids to tell stories. Schools both public and private had student exchanges. And of course there was Samantha Smith.

Mikhail Gorbachev's book, "Perestroika," mentions the Volga Peace Cruise, which was the brainchild of a Connecticut couple, as an example of how ordinary people can get together and start overcoming prejudices and misconceptions.

When President Eisenhower advocated a "people-to-people" movement back in the fifties, he didn't realize how right he was. People meeting people really works. Here's a local example:

Some Soviet teens were going to be visiting Greenfield, and it coincided with a Memorial Day parade. The visit organizers, perhaps foolishly, suggested that the Soviet teens march in the parade.

The veterans were horrified. "Totally inappropriate," they said in shocked tones, and the idea was withdrawn.

But then something strange happened. The Soviet teens came to town and stayed with local families. They visited schools and stores and hung out wherever it is Greenfield teens hang out, and on the day of the parade, they went along to watch.

And the veterans got mellow. They agreed it would be all right for the Soviet teenagers' presence to be noted.

One of the officials welcomed the kids to Greenfield and said "They all look like our own youngsters. We are all one world, with the same joys and aspirations."

In reply, one of the adults with the Soviet teens said, "We have brought you our most precious gift, our children."

Then the leader of the veterans presented the kids with an American flag and offered a "hope for peaceful coexistence."

I don't know if there were any dry eyes in town by that time. It was a moving moment, and I was really proud of those veterans for being big-hearted enough to rise above all those years of hate and distrust we've all been through.

Multiply this by thousands and you'll see why, somewhere along the way, the cold war started melting, the iron curtain started getting rusty. It was individual Americans who accomplished that, not governments or armies. And that's the story of the decade.

It may never get into the history books, but to me it's an amazing story. By taking action, these Americans may well have empowered those Eastern Europeans who are now also standing up for what they believe in.

This is what democracy is all about, and it's this courage of our democratic convictions, not Pentagon invasions, that makes America great in the eyes of the world.

56

Northampton held its first Native American powwow one August weekend at the fairgrounds -- another indication of the increasing interest in the "First Nations" people and their ways.

It's hard to find an acceptable term to cover all Native Americans. The Cherokee prefer to be called Cherokee, the Hopi Hopi, and so on through the hundreds of disparate tribes that inhabit these continents. You would think that Native American was preferable to Indian. "The only reason we're called Indians is because Columbus got lost, and thought he was in India," as one of them said. "Why should we put up with that?"

But actually, a survey among them showed a majority prefer to be called "American Indian."

Booths where you could buy silver and turquoise jewelry, feather hair ornaments, bows (but no arrows), and other arts and crafts competed with the exotic feathered costumes in the dance circle.

Meanwhile, stealing the show as far as I was concerned, were two little girls in fringed American Indian dress, dancing barefoot on the grass outside.

"Honor the Earth" was the theme of the powwow. Isn't it amazing to see how "Anglo" thought is swinging at long last around toward the American Indian attitudes on preservation of the environment, and also toward the spiritual, holistic and natural as embodied both in Native American and New Age philosophy? Makes you wonder if the earth itself is speaking to us -- although it has taken a few centuries for us to listen.

Northampton was the second powwow I attended. The first was in Grafton, Mass., a smaller, single-tribe (Hassanamisco Nipmuc) gathering that had a family feeling, in spite of the fact that cars lined the road for a couple of miles. Local and visiting as well as Hassanamisco Nipmuc families walked cheerfully up the hill to the four-acre reservation which I believe is the only piece of land in Massachusetts which has never belonged to the white man.

There was a modest entrance fee of $2, a food booth and several others with the inevitable American Indian crafts, souvenirs and books. One table had free information, including a twelve-page booklet listing numerous powwows in New England, including some nearby ones at Indian Plaza, Charlemont, and at Buffalo Village Store, Plainfield. Peacework Galleries on Main Street has additional copies of the powwow listing.

And to think that a couple of months ago in Arizona a Navajo jeweler asked me about powwows in the East and I'd never heard of such a thing.

A natural amphitheater allowed people to sit on the grass or stand to watch the dancing around the council fire. There were five drummers drumming, and a PA system which rather spoiled the pre-Columbian effect.

The MC was friendly and kindly. About 50 people, most dressed in American Indian costume, danced in a large circle around the "council fire." Dancing meant mostly a shuffle, with a few turns. One youth with forehead painted red seemed to be the major domo, raising his stick a few beats before the end so dancers and drummers could end together.

One ceremony I particularly liked was when several young people were brought forward to present their new tribal names to the elders. After the elders discussed and then accepted the names, the new Walking Bear, Thunderhawk, Wind Blossom and others were led around the circle and brought back to the chief.

After they had all been accepted, they danced around the circle to the beat of the drums.

It's certain to have made the young people feel they belonged to the community and were important. It seems too bad we Anglos don't have anything similar, except perhaps for religious events. Do we ever let our kids know they belong to a wider community, which accepts and values them?

Maybe this is one more thing we could learn from the deeper wisdom of the native people who discovered Columbus back in 1492, but knew where they were a lot better than he did.

57

I went to a church supper the other night for the first time in many a year. The very thought of going to one took me back to my childhood. Maybe that's why they're listed under "pastimes" in Hampshire Life.

It seems they haven't changed much over the years, except perhaps in price. The long tables, the cheerful volunteer waitresses, the groaning board, the mix of congregation and stranger, seemed very familiar still. I always thought it was a good idea, and I guess churches think so, too.

The one I went to was at the Methodist Church out on Route 66, but there have been lots of them advertized lately -- chicken salad and asparagus in North Hadley, roast beef in South Deerfield, a pancake breakfast in Sunderland; ham, potato salad and strawberry shortcake in Whately, Chesterfield, and Southampton. Obviously, ham and potato salad is a popular combination, but so too is asparagus and strawberries. Williamsburg offered them all.

Most of these seem to be Congregational suppers. Perhaps they're the ones who most enjoy congregating. But the Methodist one I went to offered roast turkey and all the fixin's, and Amherst Methodists went for cold roast beef and turkey.

Holy Trinity Church in Hatfield also gets into the act, though, with a combination of chicken barbecue and polkafest.

It isn't just the congregation that attends these suppers. The combination of down-home cooking, moderate price, and friendly atmosphere pulls in friends, neighbors, and downright strangers from distant towns.

We find a place at one of the long trestle tables, and ever-cheerful parishioners parcel out the turkey, the stuffing, the baked potatoes, the salad, and several kinds of vegetables. I think there was gravy, too, but I averted my eyes. Coffee, of course, and -- wonder of wonders -- seconds. Dessert may be a wide choice, which you can pick up at another table.

The church, which I hadn't visited before, is in country surroundings, so the view as we ate was of peaceful woodlands, certainly a plus.

Some may be there solely to eat, but most introduce themselves to their neighbors at the table. Perhaps the "church" aspect of the supper is a little inhibiting, since conversation tends to stay on superficial topics such as the weather. No deep discussions of philosophy or politics here. The flip side is that no dishes get thrown, either.

The ambience may not be very romantic, and of course no alcohol is served, but the feeling of community is strong, and that's something that's often missing in our lives these days.

I remember church suppers in my younger years, in Maine. We kids didn't have to sit with our parents -- they were usually busy in the kitchen -- but we were on our best behavior, and feeling very grown up. The meal seemed especially memorable, perhaps because we knew there would be no dishes for us to wash afterwards.

Strawberry shortcake, pumpkin pie with real whipped cream, blueberry cobbler, rhubarb pie; it's the desserts that stay with me, in more ways than one.

As I grew older, I'd be allowed to squeeze up and down the long aisles between tables of happy gourmands, answering cries for more potatoes or gravy or winter squash. Even the kitchen, not usually my favorite room because of the work that was usually waiting there, seemed exciting with everyone bustling busily about and steam and aromas wafting through the air.

Some churches concentrate on one or two special church suppers during the year, perhaps spring and fall. Others seem to have them every month. As long as the volunteers are willing, it must be a good way to socialize, have a meal out, reach out into the community, and make a little money, all at the same time.

More asparagus, please?

58

Walking around Beacon Hill this summer, my brother and I found ourselves outside the Boston Athenaeum, that lovely old place. I couldn't help but go in. Libraries have always drawn me like a magnet.

Northamptonites may not realize how lucky we are to have Forbes Library. I read a great many books -- not very intellectual ones, alas, mostly for entertainment -- so when I find myself in a place with an inadequate library, I start getting testy.

Much as I loved Cullen, the town where we lived in Scotland, the library there was open only three times a week, for a total of about six hours. Not only that, it had a very small selection, which was rotated now and then from the main branch 22 miles away in Elgin. Needless to say, I started going to Elgin.

There was also, the first few years we were there, an historical library in neighboring Portsoy. I was delighted to find it, and they greeted me with open arms because hardly anyone ever went there. They even allowed me to take reference books home, which will shock librarians everywhere.

Living in a large city, where the library may have a closed-stack system, is also a drag. At Forbes (which is open-stack), you can look up a book you've heard about, and then browse around it for other books on the same subject. In closed-stack systems, you make out a card for the book you've heard of, then wait and wait for a dogsbody to bring the book to you; it's a long, long process to find out what else the library might have.

The whole idea of a public library is so sane and sensible: since most of us can't afford to have huge libraries, we buy the books collectively and take turns reading them. It's a marvelous system.

Forbes, which has been around some hundred years, has 240,000 items (some tapes etc. besides books), and gets ripped off to the tune of nearly 16 items a week. The number has gone down some since they installed the security system, but that's still some 800 items per year.

It makes me angry when people abuse a system that should benefit everyone. When auditing some courses at one of the local colleges, I was told that highly competitive students will sometimes steal the library copies of a required textbook, in order to have an edge over the many students who then never get a chance to see the copy at all. As my kids might say, what kind of slime-bag would do that? And how does that skew grades in favor of the unscrupulous?

I'm sure that when communities first got together to decide on a library, they understood and accepted that this was by the people and for the people. Stealing from a library would be stealing from oneself as well as from one's friends and neighbors. Not so now, apparently. We're failing to make sure our kids learn social responsibility.

Not that I have a right to talk. My kids don't have haloes, and I'm ashamed and embarrassed to have to admit that two of them have been rather cavalier about library books, when they were young and foolish.

One of my sons ran up a $75 bill in unreturned books at Forbes. When I found out about it and confronted him, he didn't seem too interested in doing anything about it. If they were going to get returned it was apparently up to me to do it, irritating though that was. It took me several weeks before I found them all, and by the last one I was so embarrassed about it, I pulled a reverse ploy and sneaked it into the stacks without saying anything. The fact that it was a book on sex had nothing to do with it.

Later, I was helping another son move from one house to another in Boston, and discovered that he had about four boxes of books from Boston Public Library. I got out my whip and told him he could just leave them inside the library door, he didn't have to confess, but back they were going. And I stood over him until the deed was done. They're both more mature now, I hope.

What makes kids behave like that? Well, not just kids; I've seen adults helping themselves to books people donated to the League of Women Voters booksale. I think the donors intended something different.

Has it really become part of the American mentality that if we want something, we shouldn't have to deny ourselves? That anything that's easy to steal, was meant to be stolen?

If Forbes has to close its stacks, or even go out of business, because of this attitude, I know I won't be the only person around to regret it mightily.

59

See if you can guess where this route is going by the sights you can find along the way:
A painting of an apple -- or is it a tomato?
Something with a Latin name.
A cottage with hanging plants all along the roof edge.
A windmill.
A plastic Quonset greenhouse.
A row of yellow snow-plow blades.
A painting of a strawberry -- or is it a tomato?
A flagpole in a flowerpot.
A circular garden with a maple tree in the middle.
An early US flag pinned to a house.
A weathervane depicting an old-fashioned car.
A house with a half-green roof.
A POW-MIA flag.
A wishing well with flowers.
A wishing well without flowers.
A tree house.
A cattle crossing.
Power lines.
A cemetery with a nice stone wall.
A hat hanging on a door.
A new barn.
A quote from the Gettysburg Address.
You have now arrived in a town a mere 10 miles from Northampton, though the road is much prettier

and more peaceful than the traffic-laden route 9 to Amherst.

Instead of malls and car lots, you travel through woods, past tiger lilies and red barns, boat lots and a marina, views of the Connecticut River, Skinner State Park and the Holyoke Range.

You also pass a sign that says "five and a half feet deep in my living room," with other high-water marks from 1927, '36, '38, and '84. This is a dead giveaway for most people who have lived around here, though there may be newcomers who have missed this historic marker near Mitch's Marina, on the way to -- you must have guessed it by now -- South Hadley.

South Hadley is a pretty place, but one that I haven't spent much time in. I've taken my kids to summer theater there, attended writers' workshops, visited friends; and I used to go through it when I had business in Ludlow. Even now, Morgan Street conjures up a sense of adventure, since the way across country to Ludlow takes a map and compass, and I got lost many times looking for the best route.

I wandered down to South Hadley last week just to take a fresher look, and enjoyed walking around the Village Commons. There's a beautiful craft shop, several clothing boutiques and eateries, the Odyssey Bookshop, and a place called Fiddlesticks, with "objets de fun."

The Commons is a nice layout, a little reminiscent of Mongoose Junction in Cruz Bay (Virgin Islands), but I missed something that made Mongoose Junction so special: shade, plants, greenery.

It seems strange, in this five-college sommunity we live in, that there is so much more traffic between Amherst and Northampton than there is toward Mount Holyoke. But this seems headed for an inevitable change. Not only has South Hadley joined Northampton and Amherst as part of the purview of the

Daily Hampshire Gazette, but Northampton has been pasted onto South Hadley politically.

So give your kids the list of things to watch for, pile in the car, and head for South Hadley next time you feel like going someplace new. Who can find the log cabin off in the trees? At least, I think that's what I saw.

60

There were no other adults in sight last week when the quite small girl came wandering toward me down the aisle of a supermarket on King Street.

"Hi," I said. "You haven't lost your mommy, have you?"

"No... yes." The lower lip trembled ever so slightly.

"Well... let's go up to the main desk and they'll announce it over the loudspeaker, okay?"

"Okay." She put her hand trustingly in mine and I took her up to the courtesy desk, getting some necessary information on the way.

"This is Jennifer," I told the clerk at the desk. "She's three and three-quarters years old, and she's lost her mom."

The loudspeaker crackled, and a woman with an embarrassed expression started towards us.

"Is that your mom?" I asked.

"No... yes."

It turns out the hesitancy was because this was her "grandmother's child," her aunt, not her mom, but no problem. We waved goodbye, and I walked away smiling, feeling good. Little did I know that I'd run into her again that very afternoon, swimming in Leeds. It's a small you-know-what.

I know the theory is that kids today have to be taught not to talk to strangers, but it's really very pleasant when the 90 percent of us who aren't danger-

ous get a chance to have a chat with a nice little
kid.

Years ago, in Cambridge, I was friendly with a
woman who had five girls, all under the age of six.
I had been to her house frequently, but always in
the evening when the kids were asleep. I had seen
them, but they hadn't seen me.

One day I met four of them on the street, recognized them, and said hello. Immediately the six-
year-old organized her troops into a solid phalanx,
stared hard at me and said, "We don't know you."

I explained that I knew her parents, but she was
still suspicious. "Then you should know we aren't
allowed to talk to strangers," she said accusingly.
I walked away feeling intimidated, and a little angry
that our kids have to be brought up to feel alienated
from all the grownups around them. It assuredly
isn't as healthy as growing up in a community where
we can trust each other.

Lost kids provide a great opportunity for satisfying that yearning for a more trusting community,
and I've been lucky -- it's happened to me before.

I was at a conference at Silver Bay, on Lake
George in New York State, and one evening came
across a small boy with a large dead fish clutched
tightly in his hand. He was about four, and the fish
was at least half his height. He seemed to have no
one with him, so I asked if I could help.

It turns out his parents were in two different
meetings, and each thought the other had their son,
whose name was Evan. Having found the fish by the
shore, he wanted to show it to his parents, and to
have it cooked for his breakfast in the morning. I
thought I could probably trust his mother -- or any
sane person -- to squash this idea, as the fish
already had a pretty strong pong, so I said only
admiring things about his dead friend.

We found out where his mother was supposed to be, and went there, but couldn't find her. We found out where his father was supposed to be, and went there, but couldn't find him, either. We went to the rooms where they were staying, but all was quiet and empty.

By this time it was nearly dark, I was carrying Evan, and the fish was dangling wetly and stinkily down my back. Rather wearily I took Evan back to the main hall --and as we walked in the door, there was his mother.

Evan and fish were transferred to her, Evan nearly asleep but still clinging tightly to his prize, which was getting stronger every minute.

This tale, too, had a coincidental twist. At the beginning of the conference we had drawn names from a hat to be our "secret pal," and the one who had drawn my name, and had anonymously treated me to ice cream cones and other goodies all during the week, was -- Evan's dad.

61

Here's a question for you. Do you recognize these names: Pega, Bega, Tatwin, Tusketyl, Betelin, Bartholomew, Guthlac? It's almost a litany, isn't it -- almost music.

There's at least one local person who knows -- Jane Yolen of Hatfield, author of (among many others) "Ring Out: a book of bells."

That's right, Pega, Bega et al are bells, the first set of tuned bells, hung in the eighth century in Croyland Abbey.

Far closer to home are the bells which hang in the Performing Arts Center tower at Smith College. If you've ever wanted to hear the ancient art of change-ringing, these bells will be rung the afternoon of Tuesday, June 8, by the Ancient Society of College Youths from England, a crack team who have rung changes on such famous bells as those of St. Paul's Cathedral and Westminster Abbey.

Change ringing is based less on musicality than on mathematical sequences in the pattern of ringing, which explains why math departments are often more involved than music departments.

Smith owes its set of change bells to Alice Dickinson, a former math professor at Smith, and her husband David, who taught math at UMass. The Dickinsons had learned change ringing in England, and when Smith was building the Performing Arts Center, the couple looked at the tower under construction and thought, "what a great place for a set of bells!" At their urging, construction on the tower was halted until a set of bells could be installed.

Change ringing is an acquired taste, and new-comers to the art may not want to listen for the entire two and a half hours, but if you're around Smith College when change-ringing is going on, lend an ear.

If you're more musically inclined, make a note that an entirely different set of bells, the carillon bells in the clock tower at Smith, will be pealing Monday nights at 7 for five weeks in June and July.

I've always been fascinated by bells. As a child I must confess I didn't like going to church, but I liked hearing the bells ringing. In fact, occasionally the bell-ringer would let me make a feeble attempt at pulling the heavy rope. That was only because I had a special privilege -- I was the minister's daughter.

Not too long ago, I learned to play the hand-bells. First up in Pelham, but that was too far to go for the practice sessions; and then at Edwards Church.

It's an entirely different musical experience to play handbells. Usually you are playing different notes on an instrument, but with handbells, you wait for the right note to come to you, and then you play just that one. Or sometimes you have one in each hand and a sharp or flat waiting nearby. In any case, it gives a new perspective.

It's a beautiful sound, and I particularly like it when we swing the bells down and behind us, for an exciting variation that sounds like waterfalls.

Once I threatened to get a set of bells to play, and my husband counter-threatened "if you get one more instrument, I'm leaving." He was smiling, but I didn't push it.

In Cullen, Scotland, a friend gave me a brass bell with a lovely, cloister-like tone. But in

Cullen there was another use for bells that I looked at a bit askance: the night before a wedding, the bridegroom was taken out of his house by so-called friends, stripped to his shorts, covered with oil, paraded through town with a handcart and bell, and then thrown into the harbor. When my youngest was going to Scotland to be married, I warned him not to stay in Cullen the night before. He laughed, but took the hint.

Russia and the US both have famous, big, 18th century bells that I've seen and touched. Our Liberty Bell in Philadelphia, of course, and "Tsar Kolokol" in Moscow -- at 193 tons the largest ever made. But like many things that are too large, both are faulty. The Liberty Bell is cracked, and the Tsar Kolokol has a big chunk broken out of it. In fact, the Tsar was apparently never rung at all. It sits in a public square now, with kids running in and out of the hole. A strange come-down for a tsar.

When my mother was assistant minister at King's Chapel in Boston, I loved the Paul Revere bell it had. Cast in 1817, it was said by Revere to be "the sweetest bell we ever made."

But perhaps the best bell sound I ever heard wasn't even a bell. It was Pete Seeger, at John M. Greene Hall, playing "The Bells of London Town" on a 12-string guitar. You know the one, "Oranges and lemons sing the bells of St. Clemons..." Man, it was fantastic. Pega, Bega, Tatwin, Tusketyl, Betelin, Bartholomew and Guthlac would have been proud.

63

I've always been fascinated with bookstores. I even met my first husband in one. So the recent incursion of several more bookstores into Northampton has been exciting. Is Northampton going to become a mecca for booklovers as well as for restaurant-goers?

Several of the new small shops are in my neighborhood, which means I now have to leave my money at home when I go for a walk down Market Street.

Gabriel has a fascinating selection of old books. Metropolitan, near by, is well worth the walk up the stairs. Hampshire Books and Prints seems in the process of moving in. But all of these have Market Street's laid-back attitude towards hours -- they open at 10, 11, or even 12 o'clock, are apt to close at four and to take some days off.

Carousel Books, around the corner in the little plaza across from the post office, has a special place in my heart because they asked me to do a book-signing there for their grand opening. I had gone with some trepidation, because I thought I hated book-signings, but they made this one quite pleasant.

Raven Used Books, on Old South Street, has a pleasantly cool lower level space. Journey to Serenity, on the way to Florence, I just noticed yesterday. And of course there's Bookends, Ed Shanahan's venture in Florence, which by now is one of the established, rather than new, bookshops. Look in their window for some recently acquired black kittens.

Haymarket Bookstore Cafe has also been around for a while, but it does have a new, though tiny, entrance onto Main Street now, right next door to Beyond Words. It still has, but uses less, the back entrance on Amber Lane, down Crackerbarrel Alley by the parking lot -- an entrance that made you wonder if you had to say "Joe sent me" to get in.

Back in the 60s, the two bookstore giants in town were the Quill, at the far end of Green Street, and Hampshire Books, across Crafts Avenue from City Hall, in the space now occupied by Tripod Audio and some law offices. I don't think the new Hampshire Books on Market Street is any relation.

The Quill was like a university bookstore, with textbooks, college sweat shirts and mugs, calendars, and a good selection of new books. Hampshire had a Dickensian quality -- maybe it was the lovely multi-paned windows, which are still there.

Green Street was actually without a bookstore for a while, but now sports at least two -- Grecourt Bookshop, which is similar to the old Quill, and Just Books, which is even more laid back than Market Street, advertising that it is open "by chance or by appointment." A sign in the window also advertises that they have no best sellers, no T-shirts, no dancing, no videos, no fluorescence, no poetry readings, no magazines, no parties, no cafe, no neon, and that Seth's vacation has been extended. Hm.

Nowadays the two major downtown book emporia are Broadside and Beyond Words, both long-time Main Street attractions, with the Globe on Pleasant Street running a close third.

Broadside, which I've always found especially helpful, still has the edge on informal readings, where in a pleasantly bohemian atmosphere people sit on the floor and have a chance to meet authors and hear them read from their own works.

Broadside is also one of the few bookstores in the area without additional side lines -- there it's books, the whole books, and nothing but the books.

Beyond Words, which used to be in Thornes, now has a light and spacious, beautifully designed space across the street from its former location, and is the place to go for new age books and gifts.

And for longevity alone, one should mention the Old Book Store, a mecca for used books which has occupied a basement on Masonic Street for donkey's years.

I'm sure I must be leaving out several worthy bookstores, and forgetting good ones that have come and gone over the years. And a few specialty shops which also sell some books, like the American Indian selections at Peace Work Gallery.

What's exciting to me, though, is the number and variety of bookstores that Northampton has recently sprouted.

Several years ago, a British friend asked me to find a copy of John Greenleaf Whittier's poetry. I phoned all the bookstores, and found that there were three copies in the area, but they were all in Amherst. I don't think that would happen today, although Amherst has some fine bookstores, too.

My personal all-time favorite is the Book Barn, near Philadelphia, a gigantic barn filled with more nooks and crannies than an English muffin: a maze of sudden tiny lofts, with little rickety stairs, dark corners, tilting floors, low lintels, and a zillion used books in every possible field. People stagger out of there needing a new bookcase. It's irresistible. When I actually found one of my own books in there, I felt I had it made.

I remember how disappointed I was in our village in Scotland to discover that when residents told us there was a bookshop in town, they meant that up at the chemist's, over among the beach balls, cosmetics, and charm bracelets, there was a three-foot bookcase with a few books on Scotland, some maps, and a rasher of bodice-ripping paperback romances. For real books, one had to go 60 miles to Aberdeen.

London has had some fabulous bookstores, but the one I've begun visiting regularly there is Dillon's, which is huge, computerized, busy, and helpful. It was there I ordered the book on Ibn Batuta, the famed Arabian traveler of the 14th century, which I'd been unable to find anywhere else.

Across the world in Hong Kong, Swindon's has a large selection of books, many of them in English, about the Orient. As an example, I bought two photo books of China, a Chinese-English dictionary, a Chinese train time-table, and a children's beginner's book on learning Chinese characters.

But even without the oriental atmosphere, you would always know where you were anyway, because Hong Kong clerks are notoriously impolite and unhelpful, and Swindon's is no exception.

In fact, Swindon's makes you really appreciate Northampton bookshops.

Long may they prosper.

64

When the snow gets heavy and sets in for the winter's duration, that's when I most miss the land we used to own up in Goshen.

I had always wanted to own a piece of woods, and although we had several cherry trees in our back yard in Florence, that wasn't really what I'd had in mind. My husband Alec, who I think welcomed the idea of some outdoor activity, agreed, and we started looking at lots up in the nearer hilltowns.

One piece we looked at was practically vertical. Another was inaccessible except through someone else's property. Some were too big, others too small.

But the piece we found in Goshen seemed just right. It was six and two-thirds acres, lying in a pie-shaped wedge between Route 9 and the old cemetery, with maples and hemlock, rocky cliffs of garnet-strewn mica schist, a little brook, and enough space to get nearly lost in, but never quite.

There was a small plateau just a little way in from Route 9, where we always thought we might build, but never got around to it. It had already been a focal point for some previous owner, however, because there was a big old outdoor fieldstone fireplace there, and a rotting pile of logs lined up along the stone wall.

Alec got hold of a couple of huge wooden cable reels, and we rolled them up there to use for picnic tables. He even got electricity brought in to a nearby tree, though I don't think we ever tapped into it.

Our older sons used to love it up there, too. The boys and I would build bridges across the brook, climb trees, look for rock samples, make maps, and go exploring, while Alec would get out his chain saw and hack away at the felled timber and underbrush. One summer we even cut down poles and built the frame for an Indian teepee; typically, we never finished it off.

After we bought a woodstove, the chain saw got used in earnest, supplying our house in Florence with fuel for a couple of winters, and I didn't learn until much later that there had nearly been a nasty accident with that monstrous saw.

Way back, along the cemetery wall, there were some apple trees, and I couldn't decide which fantasy I preferred -- that visitors to the cemetery had flung their apple cores over our wall, or that Johnny Appleseed had come by on his way to Ohio.

There were a couple of drawbacks. The rocky underpinnings probably would not have yielded a perc test that would allow building; we never did find out. And the lovely little brook that gurgled so tunefully between snow banks from November to April, dried up in the summer just when you wanted it most.

But it was a cool place to escape to in July and August, especially with Highland Lake within walking distance. It was a favorite place to gather running pine for Christmas wreaths in December. There was at least one Boy Scout encampment up there when the boys were in the Florence troop, and we had plenty of picnics and marshmallow roasts.

Our next-door neighbor showed us the locally-famous counterfeiters' cave, which especially intrigued the boys, though the neighbor made them solemnly promise not to fool around there, since it was unsafe.

But I was especially fond of the place in winter. We would struggle up the incline to our plateau through the heavy snow, and look around in wonder at the laden trees, breathe in the sharp clean air, and stand in silence for a moment, somewhat awed by the cathedral-like stillness of the forest all around us.

It's a feeling that's harder to capture in a city, even a relatively uncrowded one like Northampton.

The place is sold now, but every time I drive past it on the way west, I give it a little salute. Especially when snow has sealed it away from casual passers-by, making it an enchanted forest for yet another winter.

65

I was in California one day last week. Well,
almost. I was phoning an 800 number there, got put
on hold, and spent nearly 40 minutes with the phone
to my ear, eavesdropping on our west coast neighbors.
It was enough to give me a tan.

Let me tell you, I'm not usually that patient
when I'm on hold. But the company I was calling was
relaying a local Los Angeles radio station over their
hold system, and I was soon fascinated by the fast-
talking guys out there who radiated sunshine and
California optimism.

When I first tuned in, I just missed the phone
number for some place where you could get a master's
degree by mail. I expect you can get almost anything
by mail in California, perhaps because you otherwise
would spend so much time caught in bumper-to-bumper
traffic.

The reason I think this is that the traffic
report was next, and very explicit -- a fatal
accident on one freeway and a truck overturned on
another had traffic backed up x number of miles --
"okay folks, the traffic on the Santa Monica is now
being freed up, moving a bit slowly at first, but
hang in there, it's almost over..."

And to think the Santa Monica had just reopened
a few days before, four months after the earthquake
damaged it. You could sense that the people in that

particular traffic jam were not even grousing. This was back to normal, and about time.

Between short bursts of rock music, the DJs advertised some local specials, including laser jet printers for $365. Boy.

Then came an ad for something I hadn't heard of before -- a new automatic busy re-dial system from GTE, whoever that is: with it you can hang up on a busy signal and the phone keeps trying automatically. The phone rings you back with a special ring when your call is going through. I suppose I'm the last one to know.

Having just had to redial numerous times to get onto this holding pattern, I figured the new system was likely to become quickly popular among impatient callers like me.

They announced Earth Day programs and projects, and not only offered prizes for various Earth activities, but also kept interspersing bits of information about pollution, trash, and smog, all of which Californians probably know rather a lot about already.

I even had a chance to eavesdrop on a pub in Dublin, Ireland. The station was having a contest, or else made that up on the spot. A random phone call in the area was matched with the pub in Dublin, and the Angeleno had 30 seconds to get the Irish barmaid to say the word "shillelagh." The poor man didn't even know what it was, and told the bar maid it was "a kind of stick -- maybe they use it for herding sheep, I don't know."

In spite of this gross ignorance, the barmaid guessed the word, and everyone cheered, including an unlikely listener in Northampton, Mass.

"You've won $1,000!" the DJ shouted to the man.

"And what do I get?" asked the barmaid in Dublin. No flies on her.

"Uh -- would you like a Z tee-shirt?"

There was a very short pause. But Irish barmaids know when not to quibble. "Sure! I don't know what it is, but sure."

This international person-to-person goodwill fling ended merrily all around, and they went back to the traffic helicopter for another report on the rush-hour traffic. I could almost see the sunshine bouncing off all that chrome.

And to top it all off, the 8:30 a.m. temperature reading was given -- a perfect 72 degrees. Ours, at 11:30, was 56. By then I was ready to hop on a plane and go. So, what's an earthquake or two?

Fortunately -- or not -- my party came on the line about then and I was yanked back to New England reality. But my imagination was still working overtime.

Hey, you in Los Angeles, here we have real seasons. You want to see snow? We still have a little up in the hills. You who always have flowers, can you appreciate as much as we do the coming of the purple crocus, the robin, the mud? Come on over and sample New England.

Or, better yet, have you got a guest room?

66

I suppose you saw in the Gazette about the nine
youths who entered a home in Belchertown last Saturday and started breaking furniture and windows.

As it happened, I had five teenaged boys in my
yard Sunday night, stripped to the waist and wearing
sweat bands around their heads. A lot of them were
sporting tattoos. They had been roaming around the
neighborhood all afternoon. Sound like more of the
same bad news? Well, you're wrong.

Seems these guys were sitting around that
morning, bemoaning the fact they had no money, and
decided to round up two lawnmowers, a weed-whacker, a
rake and a broom from their various households, and
go out looking for work.

I'm sure glad they lived on the east side of
town, where I do, because they came by at just the
right time.

I'd been letting my lawn go for far too long.
Either it was too hot, or too wet, or I was busy, or
the weeds were beginning to look pretty. But for the
past few days I'd been writing down "mow the lawn" on
my daily list of things to do, in ever larger letters,
as the excuses went on.

So when these enterprising young men appeared at
my door, in the already nearly dark at 7 p.m., and
offered to do my lawn for $10, I couldn't say no.

Boy, were they efficient. Despite one mower
quitting (they got it started again) and the weed-

whacker giving out (they got that going again, too), they zoomed over my lawn, raked it, and bagged the cuttings.

The edges along the fence, which for some reason were quite tall -- well, it's been hot -- were felled by the whacker. The sidewalks were brushed down with the broom, the gardens carefully trimmed, and they were ready to be on their way. The lawn looked better than it had since the day I moved in.

Listen, I do my best.

"Do you have a name for your group?" I asked them, wondering how I was going to contact them next time my lawn needed a scythe.

"No, we just started today. Done four lawns so far."

They told me they had started out from Williams Street, walked all over that area, carrying the equipment, and then had started going up and down the streets between Market Street and the cemetery.

In the end I gave them a bonus and, amazingly, so did my neighbor. "Hey," he said. "Any time you see a bunch of teenagers being that enterprising and useful, it ought to be encouraged."

They had cleared $65, they said. Not bad for an afternoon's work. But even more, those guys made a good name for themselves, and perhaps even for teen-agers in general; they had given their self-esteem and their pockets a shot in the arm, to mix a few metaphors. And I'd be willing to bet those five guys will always land on their feet.

Too often we read in the papers about teen gangs and violence, or hear our own teens at home wailing "But there's nothing to do!" and our opinion of teens goes down another notch.

Just thought I'd let you know there are a few around town who know better than that. Like they know an overgrown lawn when they see one.

I know it's hard for lots of people to find jobs, and particularly teens. It's simplistic to say look around for a need, and fill it. But that's the simple thing these guys did, and others could do it, too. I hope they have a good time with the money they earned, and that when they get older and have rent to pay, they remember their project.

And if we have another winter like the last one, I hope they drop by again, with shovels.

67

I've been learning a fascinating new language. For many years I've been a dilettantish dabbler in languages, not in any scholarly sense except perhaps for French, which I used to teach, but absorbing enough in a variety of tongues to carry on a short, limited conversation.

Most are European languages, but I can also count to ten in Malayan, say "I love you" in Mandarin, "Merry Christmas" in Hawaiian, "I'm hungry" in Gujarati, and "I'm about to die" in Japanese. I even learned Braille, for a blind friend who seldom uses it.

Not that any of this has been very useful. It's sort of a collection, like seashells. Sometimes very rusty seashells.

The new language I've been studying is signing. I had been reading Joanne Greenberg's books, and watching "Reasonable Doubts" on television, and then noticed that a class in signing was about to begin in Easthampton. It sounded like a good idea.

I've long admired those signers who translate simultaneously as others are speaking. It seems so expressive, so fast, so difficult. Now, when I can recognize a word here and there, it's very satisfying. And signing seems to be gaining ground. Even the Olympics had signers at the opening ceremony.

Personally, I'd like to see a universal sign language. Since many of the signs are idea-based rather than word-based, it seems as if it could happen fairly easily. People, alas, are apparently too perverse for that. Though languages keep changing, they are more likely to develop along narrower, more colloquial lines than along broader, universal ones.

Biblical legend has it that the people of the world once all spoke the same language. In Roman times every educated person spoke Latin, from England to the near East. In the last century, "Pidgin" English developed in the East as a kind of lingua franca. The Chinese, who speak different languages from province to province, can always understand each other by their ideographic writing. The American Indian tribes used signs to transcend their multiplicity of tongues. In more recent times, universal languages like Esperanto have been artificially developed.

German was the common language in the Austro-Hungarian Empire that covered much of Europe. French prevailed for several centuries in the courts of Europe; English prevailed in the British Empire on which the sun never set; and American English is popular in today's world of multinational corporations.

But for most of the world, the Tower of Babel which separates one ethnic group from another is apparently still standing.

Wouldn't it be great if we didn't have to learn umpteen languages any more in order to travel around the world, but only one -- signing? It seems a very worthwhile goal to me, and in fact a universal sign language has been put together, but it's as artificial as Esperanto and even less well-known. A pity.

We all have used sign language of sorts at one time or another. You've nodded your head, shaken your fist, pointed to what you want. Perhaps you've tapped your watch to call attention to the time, held a thumb and little finger up to your cheek in imitation of a phone, or gestured with a cupped hand for "would you like a drink." You don't have to be Italian, even Yuppies do this.

The "pidgin sign language" we've been learning is more complex than that, and quite fascinating to watch. Our class was full of laughter as we stumbled our way along. We all thought we had learned the alphabet pretty well, until we learned how fast things got finger-spelled.

Many of those in the class had relatives to practice on. The rest of us had to strut our stuff in front of a mirror.

Will I ever use it? I don't know yet. Sometimes life turns up something appropriate, sometimes not. But it satisfies some urge for expression, to be able to say "my oldest son lives in England" with my hands, even if it's only to a mirror.

There has been one moment of delighted recognition: when Tom Harkin dropped out of the presidential race at Gallaudet College for the Deaf, he was holding up his fingers in an odd way. With a sudden whoop of delight, I recognized it: he was signing "I love you."

I know and understand Clarke School for the Deaf's policy of forbidding sign language to their students. They know that if sign language is around, the students are less likely to learn to use whatever residual hearing they may have, and less likely to learn lip-reading.

Nonetheless, it does seem too bad to deprive anyone of this eloquent, beautiful language form. Especially when I need someone to practice on.

68

I ordered my first cassette from the Public
Radio Music Source the other day, and I must say it
was easy, fairly quick, and not expensive. Whoever
thought up the service had a good idea. Unless a
recording is recent and popular, it's often difficult
to find.

The recording I wanted was not of Bach or
Beethoven, but of the British musical comedienne,
Anna Russell, whose hilarious description of Wagner's
operatic Ring Cycle I heard one day on WFCR. The new
Music Source immediately identified the tape I
wanted, told me the price, and that was it.

I've been having a good belly-laugh since it
arrived. Not only the Ring story encapsulated, but
how to write your own contemporary Gilbert and
Sullivan opera, what to expect by way of introduction
if you're singing for a women's club, and several
comic arias in fractured foreign languages, by this
former operatic singer who found comedy was a quicker
road to the limelight.

Her tour de force is a quartet in which she
sings all four parts.

I've had a want list for several years, of
similar high comedic talents. I finally taped a
personal copy of Victor Borge, proabably the most
famous of this genre. And in Britain a couple of
years ago I found a two-casette collection of Gerard
Hoffnung.

If you haven't heard of him, he's the one who made famous the tragic story of the bricklayer who had a run-in with a load of bricks. And if you haven't heard that story, you've missed a masterpiece.

Hoffnung, who rather resembled Alfred Hitchcock in girth, was a musician, radio personality, writer, and cartoonist -- a real Renaissance man. However, as he said, "My artist friends say I'm a very good musician, and my musician friends say I'm a very good artist."

An example of his off-the-wall humor is that he didn't see the point of men having facial hair. It would make more sense, said he, if one could grow something useful, like watercress.

Another famous routine of Hoffnung's was reading a publicity letter from an Italian innkeeper, "There is a French widow in every bedroom, affording delightful prospects..."

Now I'm thinking of asking Music Source if they have a casette of Flanders and Swann, a team of musical comedians who were popular in Britain when we lived there. Donald Swann gave a solo performance a couple of years ago at Shelburne, part of the Mohawk Trail series. Perhaps the closest American example to Swann is Mark Russell, with musical satires on current mores and events.

And I wonder if there's a tape of Hal Holbrook as Mark Twain? When he performed here in Northampton ages ago I reviewed it for the Gazette, and was so impressed I bought his book, "Mark Twain Tonight," which contains a delicious potpourri of Twain's stories and one-liners.

Perhaps there's also a casette of Ruth Draper, whose recording of monologues I used to get from Forbes Library. Her "Italian Lesson," "At the Seaside," and other dry take-offs on English life were a great introduction to British humor.

Such a lot of good laughter is out there, waiting. Now that I've learned how to get hold of all these goodies, only my wallet is going to hold me back.

69

Northampton has a quality of the unexpected that I admire. I for one did not object to the colorful face that Ann August store once put forth, and I'm glad we're now getting gargoyles on Main Street to go with the medeival tone of our city hall. Even if most of them are ninja turtles.

That unexpectedness even extends to out of town, where you can find llama farms and ostriches being reared, salamander crossings, cow plop derbies, and the occasional moose or bear giving us the once-over, and vice versa.

In town, some of my favorite sights have included a Smithie in a long white dress and big floppy hat, rollerskating down Elm Street; a guy on a tandem with a teddy bear riding the rear seat; a weasel up a tree on Main Street; a dog riding along with his head out the sunroof, ears flapping; and our wide range of street musicians, from the band from the Andes and the guy with the steel drums, to a junior-high sax player and a tiny little girl playing the violin.

In another part of town, fading slightly, there is what is probably the world's longest hopscotch layout. Done in multi-colored chalk, it starts somewhere up Graves Avenue, turns the corner and runs along Market Street, and then -- I thought I was going to discover who was the originator of this work of art, but "home" turned out to be the laundromat.

The other day, I was downtown and realized I should make a phone call. A friend happened by, and I asked her if she knew where the nearest phone was. Did she ever -- she must be the resident expert on Northampton phones. Which ones still work on just a dime; ones where you can call all over for 50 cents; which ones to stay away from. Where every single one is located. What a lot of unexpected information we each have tucked away where nobody knows about it.

There was recently on lower Main Street, a decidedly different purple bus. Originally a school bus, this one now sported a regular house door, complete with an oval pane of glass and varnished panels.

This was an intriguing vehicle, not just because it was painted purple, but because a second storey had been added -- a truncated VW bus in front, and a little log cabin affair in the back. Park under a tree, and you have your own little treehouse to sleep in. Alice in Wonderland stuff.

"That your bus?" I asked the dark-haired woman on the sidewalk next to the bus's open door. She nodded.

More nosey questions elicited the fact that she had driven the bus all the way from Madison, Wisconsin, and that yes, the two storeys in the bus were connected inside. I didn't find out what kind of bizarre stairway she had in there. She didn't plan to stay in Northampton, but didn't know where she was going next.

There's a particular sense of freedom you feel from starting down a road with no particular goal in mind. My feet began to itch.

Then a friend told me she'd heard of a wierd new folk remedy for arthritis, involving white raisins and gin. Where on earth do these things come from, anyway? And so precise -- nine raisins a day? Perhaps the number is supposed to sound more scientific, but it just makes it sound less so, to me.

Movin' on down to the foot of Old South St., I stopped to admire the new Art Garden there, which took me back momentarily to Japan. Tiny gardens with space and simplicity, consisting of perhaps only a tree and a rock, were always pleasant surprises there.

Congratulations to whoever thought up the idea for that spot in Northampton. But hey, will someone please water those trees?

The Saturday morning farmer's market, the bike path and bridge, the new traffic lights that respond to your car in four seconds -- none of these things were around a few short years ago.

Yup, Northampton's getting more interesting. Get outdoors and take a walk around before the snows come back.

Index